BE STILL

GOD'S GRACE IS BIGGER THAN WORLDLY DECEIT

Recognizing Your Potential and Finding
Your Godly Purpose

AMANDA FILKINS

ISBN 978-1-63844-904-1 (paperback)
ISBN 978-1-63874-767-3 (hardcover)
ISBN 978-1-63844-905-8 (digital)

Christian Faith Publishing, Inc.
832 Park Avenue
Meadville, PA 16335
www.christianfaithpublishing.com

Printed in the United States of America

CONTENTS

To all of the passion seekers who know they have a purpose that is greater than them, this is for you. Go change the world.

AUTHOR'S NOTE

This book is full of vulnerability. Chapter after chapter, you will read about my struggles and how God has shown me the light through my circumstances. It is so many of my misconceptions of the world put on paper for you to see God's grace through them all. My hope is that readers can relate to my experiences and see God's love and recognize that God's way is the best way. As an imperfect person living in this broken world, my goal is not to portray perfection. I still struggle with many of these issues; however, I now try to see them through a different lens.

This book helped me to put those thoughts and ideas together and gave me a perspective on life that I will forever see. I hope to give you that same perspective. My prayer for you is that God will use these words to bring peace in your heart, show you how special you truly are, and for you to acknowledge just how perfect He really is. Through this book, I hope He speaks directly to you and that you feel His immeasurable love. I prayed my way through this thing, so God is in every chapter and in every word. I pray that you feel that and that you find what you're looking for.

INTRODUCTION

First, I want to begin by explaining what the title of this book means and where it came from. If you type *Be Still books* into the Google search bar, you get 4,480,000,000 results. I don't know that there are that many different books named *Be Still* specifically, but regardless, that is *a lot* of results. I don't know the reason behind the name of some of those books, but I do know the reason for the name of my book. And it's a very personal but powerful reason that I hope will inspire you in some way.

I was a senior in college working my way toward graduation. It was an exciting but stressful time of my life because I had no idea what my plans were afterward. I was always a planner (you'll read about this later) and had lots of ideas to go to graduate school (you'll read about this too), but nothing felt right to me. So I just kept working my way through hoping that God would open doors where I was meant to go.

During my first semester of that final year, something clicked that I had never experienced before, and my relationship with Jesus took off running. I started listening to podcasts that talked about godly purpose, and God lit a fire inside my soul. I created a blog and posted content that related to my struggles and how God was showing me different perspectives. I was going through this deep phase of transformation where God was molding my heart and changing the way I viewed the world.

The "not so pretty" side of this is that I experienced many nights of growing pains learning to trust God with my unknown future. I had to give God the pen of my life and let go of my control (And I would be lying if I said that I don't still struggle with this tremendously). I was finally able to understand what it meant to *know* that God has a plan for my life and that all I have to do is pray for direction. I also started to see that God's plan is the *best* one for me. He put me here on this planet for a specific reason and gave me talents and gifts to use to fulfill that purpose. He knows what will bring me the most joy on earth because he designed me that way. Slowly, I began to understand what it meant to surrender my ways for His ways no matter how crazy they may seem to the rest of the world.

One night, during this growing phase, I was feeling overwhelmed and confused about which direction God wanted me to go. I had experienced many days of silence, unsure of what God was trying to show me. I fell to my knees, put my palms together, and wept…and wept…and wept. I prayed for something, *anything*, that would give me peace and guidance in the direction of what God wanted me to do. Amid the tears and crying out for comfort, I felt a soft whisper, *Be still and know that I am God*. I stopped crying and started praying harder. I wanted more. But God didn't want to give me more. He wanted me to be still in the moment and let Him do His work. I needed to quiet my thoughts, soul, and life and just let God speak in whatever way He wanted to give me the kind of guidance I was asking for. I got up off my knees, dried my eyes, and took a long hot shower. I forced myself to be calm and cleared my mind the best that I could.

And then came the thoughts. This idea to write a book came out of nowhere, and the calling to do it was a feeling of intensity that I had never experienced before. I laid in bed that night and wrote the titles and ideas for every chapter without hesitation. God was crafting this book and using a nobody like me to physically put the pieces together. And the process has been so perfectly timed it blows my mind. I would experience something that would directly relate to a chapter I was writing. Or I would be struggling with the words to say something else, and I would listen to a podcast that would connect the dots for me. Things would happen in my life and teach me a lesson that I would later share in one of these chapters. I would think about writing constantly. I mean seriously all the time. If I could remember every God-moment I've had while writing this, I would share them all with you. It's been an amazing challenge that I am so blessed God laid on my heart to do.

Why am I sharing all of this? Well, I told you that I would tell you where the title of this book came from. But I also told you that I would tell you what it means.

In a world where life can sometimes feel really loud with chaos, busy schedules, restless thoughts, etc., if we want to hear God's plan, sometimes we need to slow things down and listen. If you want God's best, you have to give Him your heart in a quiet place where He can speak truth, love, and guidance into your life. And I hope by reading these chapters, you can get a little piece of that. I pray that God will use this book to nudge you in a fragile place to put you back on the path that He intended for you all along.

And to do that, I begin each chapter talking about a lie that the world tells us is true, and I end each chapter explaining how God's truth is the *real* truth. I use experiences from my own life to exemplify the misconceptions that made me feel empty while providing hope that God is so much bigger than the problems we face. I know I'm not alone facing these struggles, and I believe that God placed this book in your hands for a reason. I pray that if you resonate with any of these battles, that you find peace in the truth that follows.

God's love for you is limitless, and He truly wants the very best for your life. I pray that this book is the breakthrough you've been looking for and that it inspires you to seek your godly purpose. All I ask is that you open up your heart, mind, and soul while you read, and allow the stillness to guide you the way that it guided me.

Let God change your world.

CHAPTER 1

Your Pain Is Eternal

THE EARLY DAYS

I'm seven years old. It's Christmas morning. My parents are sound asleep, and I know my brother and sister are just as anxious as I am for them to wake up. All I can think about is the long list I gave Santa a month ago and how I feel like I can't contain the excitement that I'm feeling from head to toe to start ripping apart that wrapping paper.

My bed is on the top bunk of a bunk bed set. My five-year-old brother sleeps on the bottom bunk. My three-year-old sister has just recently upgraded to a "big girl bed" that sits just parallel to the bunk set. For the record, my parents tried to split us all up, but my brother refused to switch rooms because we were all the best of friends (most of the time).

I have been staring at the Noah's ark painting on the wall in my room for about two minutes, and then the excitement takes over. I hang my head over my bedside to check if Noah is awake yet. Of course, like I suspected, his big brown eyes are staring around the room just as mine had been a few seconds prior. We stare into each other's eyes for about half a second, and then our attention moves toward April's bed.

We are completely unamused to see our super laid-back sister in a dead sleep. Seriously? It's Christmas morning, and she's the only kid in the entire world who isn't jumping off the walls right now.

Mission number one of the morning—get April's booty out of bed.

I quietly push back my blankets and make my way down the ladder. There is about a foot of room on both sides of her bed. I tiptoe to one side. Noah is on the opposite side. We look at each other and give "the nod."

Onto the bed with full force we go—jumping and yelling loud enough for April to hear but quiet enough not to wake our parents up; we say, "It's Christmas! Get up, get up, get up!"

Startled, her eyes open wide, and she instantly starts bawling. At seven and five years old, Noah and I were not the best at recognizing that our little sister was still basically a baby.

We try to stop the crying by covering her mouth, patting her head, and trying to make stuffed animals do funny things to make her laugh. Luckily for us, the stuffed animals came through, and the tears came to an end.

Noah and I grabbed her hand and walked her into the living room where our beautifully decorated six-foot tree stood with presents sitting at every angle beneath it. April had been too young to really understand Christmas in the past, so this year was extra special. We showed her her name on some of the neatly wrapped gifts. We took her to her stocking hanging on the fireplace mantle stuffed to the top with more goodies just for her. A grin from ear to ear reflected her excitement. Noah and I were equally as excited as she was.

Now that all three of us were hyped up after seeing that Santa was indeed good to us this year, it was time to check on our parents. In our house, we were not allowed to open any presents until Mom and Dad were up and ready with the camera. It was an unamusing waiting game that we dreaded every Christmas morning. But we knew it was just the way the cookie crumbled and that Mom and Dad had all the power in the world to take these precious beauties from Santa away in an instant.

My siblings and I make our way to our mom and dad's bedroom door. We wait patiently for a whopping thirty seconds.

Creeeeak. We crack the door open just enough so that one of our tiny heads can peep in and scan the room in hopes that at least one of them is awake.

Creeeeak. We close the door extra slowly because (1) the door loves to sound like a screaming alarm system when we're trying to be quiet, and (2) we're scared that if our parents hear the obnoxious door, they might be mad at us for interrupting their sleep and perhaps cancel Christmas this year.

My siblings and I go through this process a few more times, slowly opening and closing the door, until we decide that *enough is enough.* This "patiently waiting" garbage is not going to fly on the day that all the kids of the world— including my brother, sister, and I—have been waiting for since December 26 of the previous year.

But there's a problem. If simply waking them up from the sound of the door might upset them, what in the world are they capable of if we *purposely* wake them up?

We tiptoe back into our room where I call a team meeting. I was always the plan maker in these situations. As the oldest of three, I called the shots because I had the most "wisdom" (according to me).

Mission number two of the morning—wake up our parents in the smoothest way humanly possible.

I assign roles to each of us. I was "Amanda, the door master." Then there was "Noah, the bodyguard." And last but not least, there was "April, the sweet talker."

We make our way back to the entrance of their room. I assume my role and almost in slow motion pull the door open. Step one is complete. Next, it's Noah and April's time to shine. They make their way into the dark room with only the light from the hallway to guide them. I'm keeping watch just in case the cats decide they want to intervene. I watch as they make their way to the side of the bed. Noah is scanning his surroundings "bodyguarding" against who knows what, and April is mustering up the perfect words to say.

Noah and I hold our breath as April makes a move.

Tap, tap, tap. She lightly touches our dad's shoulder. Nothing.

Tap, tap, tap. She pushes a little harder.

"Daddy…" She whispers with her sweet innocent three-year-old voice.

"Daddy… It's Christmas. Santa came. We want to open presents."

In a tired whisper, he replies, "Good morning, honey, Mom and Dad will be up shortly to make pancakes and we can start opening presents."

Wow, that was easy. Apparently, the "go back to bed" monster doesn't come out to play on Christmas.

The rest of the morning is followed by a massive pancake, eggs, and toast breakfast. We all eat together. We read the Christmas story from the Bible. We open presents one at a time (this always killed us too). Noah, April, and I loved on and hugged our parents all morning.

These were the memories that I could not wait to build upon and look back at with a happy heart. What a beautiful Christmas day and blessed family we were. It was the time of our lives.

MY WORLD CAME CRASHING DOWN

Two years later, I was nine years old. My mom and dad hadn't been getting along for a while now. There was a lot of yelling and more door slamming than I had ever remembered in the past.

Noah and I would come up with "plans" to try to make Mom and Dad stop arguing. He was seven now, so I figured he had *some* good ideas to contribute. I was always assigned to Mom because "girls will listen to girls," and he was assigned to Dad because "boys will listen to boys." We wanted to calm them down and help them remember how to love each other like they had years ago during that beautiful Christmas morning.

Obviously, our plans were not successful being that a nine- and seven-year-old don't know the first thing about (1) conflict, and (2) how to resolve conflict, especially within the context of a marriage.

I remember one specific day was a particularly loud and extra door-slamming kind of fight. My siblings and I hid in The Addition (the official name of the add-on to our house that was not finished yet). We had a guinea pig named Simon that lived in The Addition. We sat around Simon's cage. We all knew things weren't going well. I hugged my brother and sister that day with tears in my eyes. We loved our parents so deeply, but we knew that life was not about to get any better anytime soon.

I cannot remember the exact day, but I do remember the exact feeling. I believe my dad had brought me home from school that day. He had said he needed to talk to me. I knew. I didn't want to believe it, but I had a pretty good idea what he was going to tell me.

He took me into his room and sat me on the edge of the bed. He crouched down so our faces were at the same level. Tears began flooding his eyes as he was about to unleash the sad news I had hoped I would never hear.

"Mommy and Daddy have not been getting along for a while now. We are getting a divorce."

Crack. Crack. Crack. Shatter. My heart was in pieces.

Being the oldest, I had been around to witness the good years of my parents' marriage. I had felt the happy feelings, seen my parents love each other for years, and watched our house grow into a home. The whole world that I had grown up in was crumbling. I didn't understand. I was angry. I was broken. I was lost.

Being the big sister, I felt a new responsibility to do my best to be there for my siblings. Noah was old enough to know what divorce meant, but April was far too young to *really* understand what was going on.

In a nutshell, the next year or so was complete destruction. So many people would ask if I was okay or how I was doing, and although I knew people meant well, it became frustrating receiving attention about an issue that I wanted to pretend was not my reality. It was an extremely overwhelming and emotionally defeating time for a nine-year-old girl.

It was also a time when I did not understand where God was through it all. I was young and too immature to grasp the concept of a personal relationship with God, but I always grew up in church. I was baptized when I was seven and knew that Jesus died for me. I did not fully understand what it meant to be a follower of Jesus, but I did know that He was a huge part of my upbringing. I knew that God meant love and that giving my heart to Him was the happiest way to live. So if God wanted the best for me and wanted me to be happy following Him, then why were my parents getting a divorce? Why did this happen to *my* parents of all people? Why was He letting this happen to my siblings and me? Where was he? Did he even care how much I was hurting?

THE HEALER

First, let me make it *very* clear that I do not, by any means, hold resentment toward my parents for anything and everything that happened. They're human. The flesh is weak. Divorce stems from the enemy. There is nothing more exciting to Satan himself than to see a beautiful family crumble because of his influence. Sometimes Satan's voice sounds the loudest when we don't see any hope left.

I felt emotionally empty for many years after my parents officially split apart. As the kid who vividly remembered so many details about the "picture-perfect" life I had lived years before, I could not understand how and why my world had completely turned upside down. I was confused. I was a lost soul wondering where in the world this "Jesus" I was raised to worship was through all of this.

It is extremely easy to spiral into a really negative space when traumatic events happen to us. We blame family. We blame friends. We blame ourselves. And we blame God.

But do we ever stop to think about *where* these awful things come from? Sometimes bad things happen to good people that we don't understand, but who ultimately benefits when we allow these horrible incidents to transform our minds for the worst? Who is the one that thrives in your pain and finds the utmost joy in grabbing a hold of your heart to draw you closer to more excruciating suffering? I can tell you all day, all night, all year, and all of my lifetime that it most certainly isn't our loving Father.

Our world has shifted into this mindset of "divorce is normal," "depression is normal," and "life sucking is normal." We have chosen to accept the increasing divorce rates and rise in depression diagnoses. We think of happiness as a rarity.

No, no, and *no*. God *never* intended for our world to be this way.

> Trust in the Lord, and do good; dwell in the land and befriend faithfulness. Delight yourself in the Lord, and he will give you the desires of your heart. (Psalm 37:3–4)

> Our mouths were filled with laughter, our tongues with songs of joy. Then it was said among the nations, "The Lord has done great things for them." (Psalm 126:2)

> God saw all that he had made, and it was very good. And there was evening, and

there was morning—the sixth day.
(Genesis 1:31)

> You were not created to carry heavy chains. You are more than your bad situation. You don't have to go through it alone.

Joy, the desires of our hearts, laughter, great things—all of which God wants for us and created the world to be. He made it to be a *good* place.

You were not created to carry heavy chains. You are more than your bad situation. You don't have to go through it alone. You are a beautiful child who got an unlucky draw. But God is a marvelous healer if you simply allow Him the opportunity to surround your heart with the love and mercy He so eagerly wants to give you.

It has taken me a long time to *really* understand God's healing motives and His tremendous interest and love for my life. But wow, I am a completely different woman because I *did* make the choice to follow Him and allow Him to take the chains off my back and use them for good (a.k.a. this book). I would not be sharing this testimony without the overwhelming presence and blessings God has brought me through my decision to lay my heartache at His feet.

Then the Lord your God will bring you to the land which your fathers possessed, and

you shall possess it. He will prosper you
and multiply you more than your fathers.
And the Lord your God will circumcise
your heart and the heart of your descen-
dants, to love the Lord your God with all
your heart and with all your soul, that you
may live. (Deuteronomy 30:5–6)

The beautiful thing about your mess is that He has a
plan to use it for good. That might be the hardest thing to
understand in the heat of the battle, but He promises not
to leave you. He *will* make up for your loss. Your suffering
will be restored, and your story will be used for His great
plan. Love and trust Him, and He will take care of the rest.

Now some of you may be reading this and thinking,
*Well, my parents are still happily married, so this doesn't apply
to me at all,* or *divorce definitely sucks, but my life has been so
much more unkind to me.* So let me ask you, *What is your
story?* My traumatic event was an ugly divorce. Yours might
be alcoholism in the home, a form of abuse, a tragic family
death, or whatever else you have dealt with. Trauma is
trauma, and it comes in many forms and affects us in a
wide range of ways.

We all have a story.

Weaknesses are commonalities. We
feel connected to one another through
being vulnerable about our difficulties.
We all have insecurities that stem from
somewhere or something. We were not
simply born with them. We have struggles that we hold

close to our hearts that have influenced the way that we act or see the world today. We all have a story.

My point is that each and every one of these incidents in our lives has an enormous impact on us, and we *all* have them. We might not even realize that we've been impacted by an event, and we just assume that living with the consequences of that problem are normal. But it does not have to be your normal, and we don't have to let it consume our hearts, minds, or actions because we have a healing Father who wants to take the pain and heal our hearts.

We cannot control every unfortunate thing that happens to us; however, we *can* control how we respond. We can allow it to control our lives and emotions, or we can control the way we view it, give it to God in prayer, and fight for a better tomorrow.

Jesus provides hope, peace, forgiveness, and strength—things we often need when we are hurting. We need hope to rest assured that our life *does* have a purpose and a future despite our current circumstances. We need peace to have the ability to sit in our houses at ten o'clock on a weekday night in complete utter quiet and feel contentment in our hearts. We need forgiveness for perhaps ourselves or to forgive those who have hurt us in ways we have not been able to move past. We need strength to help fight the battle we're facing physically and/or mentally.

Do you feel stuck? Angry? Depressed? Empty? Alone? Confused? Well I am here to tell you that God has no desire for that in your life. The world might tell you that what happened to you is "normal," and although we live in a fallen place and the temporary emotions exist because we're human, the result of your situation does not have to end in constant suffering. He has a *much* bigger and more purposeful meaning for you. He wants to give you the tools to manage and get past your hurt and flood your heart and soul with His healing power. He wants to fulfill you. He wants the absolute best for you. He wants to use you and your situation for His beautiful good.

The question is, will you let Him?

CHAPTER 2

Earthly Satisfaction Will Fulfill

FUN OR RUN

"*They're here!*" A boy with a familiar face raced past me waving his arms rapidly back and forth to draw attention. I immediately turned and saw the terror consuming my friend's face. Without hesitation, my legs took off in a dead sprint.

The second I saw the massive bonfire, I screamed. "*Everyone, out now!*"

I always knew memorial weekend was a sketchy time to be out drinking, especially as an underage kid. But being an eighteen-year-old fresh graduate, I was "invincible" and thought it was worth the risk. A gut feeling haunted my conscience, but I chose to ignore the warning sign and gave in to peer pressure. Off came the bottle caps and down went the alcohol. The burning sensation running down my throat was not a foreign feeling, and it always felt so worth it. I was completely unaware or perhaps in denial of the irresponsibility of my current actions. Little did I know the consequences that I would face in the eventful night I was about to encounter.

Music blaring, wind blowing through my hair, and drinks in hand, I was living the "teenage dream." I had graduated about a week ago, and naturally, an "appropriate" celebration had to take place. A large group of us piled into the car, and off we went in search of a good time.

As the car came to a halt, my heart raced. We had arrived at this place where the "cool kids" hung out and that was enough explanation for me. A few drinks on the ride over had my world spinning. Struggling with every movement, I dragged my weight out of the vehicle. Everywhere I looked became hazier. With extra concentration, I successfully made it through the cave-like path, canopied by trees, to the comfort of familiar friends circling an enormous fire.

This place we called "The Pit" was an exciting and, more importantly, a *secret* place to party. There was a long dirt path to get back to the main area that was surrounded by woods. It was a large gravel pit with the perfect center for a bonfire. We were country kids, so yes, a gravel pit was *the place* to go.

I was thrilled that it was going to be a wild night. Creating conversation with anyone I encountered, I was having an exciting evening until I turned my bottle upside down and realized I was in need of drink number "who knows, I lost count."

"Jessica!" I obnoxiously yelled.

I linked my arms in hers and began the voyage back to the car. She too was under the influence, so no questions asked, onward and forward we went. We were about halfway there when he came frantically dashing past us.

"*They're here!*" He shrieked. "*Cops! They're here! Run!*"

I felt a rush of adrenaline consume every muscle in my body, and I took off. So many thoughts were running through my head. *Why did I do this? What if I don't get away? What will I do if I get caught? How will this affect my future?*

"*Everyone, out now! The cops are here!*" I screeched, making my way through the swarm of minors. Everyone darted in a frantic search for any hiding place they could find.

I continued to run through the thick woods until a large tree branch in my path brought me to my knees. I was in complete darkness. I had no clue where anyone else might be. Using my hands to feel and guide me forward, I made my way to a tree that I could rest my back against and think. I squeezed my hand in my pocket and pulled out my only resource: my cell phone. With only five percent left, I had to act fast. Elizabeth, one of my best friends in high school, would have my back. I found her name in my contacts and pressed the call button. The phone rang for what felt like hours. My patience was growing slim.

Four percent remaining.

Voicemail.

Three percent remaining.

Voicemail.

Two percent remaining.

Finally.

"Liz, I'm deep in the woods. I don't know what to do."

"Come back to the fire. It was a false alarm."

"Are you *sure?*"

"Yes, I'm sure. It's all fine. Get back here."

I took a deep breath and pulled myself up to my feet. Trudging through the mud and sticks, feet cut up, I finally made my way back. Fear was still the center of my attention. I had a knot in my gut the size of a planet.

"We have to get out of here," I nervously whispered to Liz the moment I saw her. "I have a horrible feeling about all of this."

I had more than a horrible feeling. People don't scream cop warnings for no reason. I just knew something *really bad* was going to happen that night.

"You think so?" Elizabeth questioned.

"Yeah, I *absolutely* think so. I think we need to leave."

She knew we should all stick together, so she agreed. I looked around at the group of friends that I had come here with and noticed one girl missing. Stephanie must have found a way out when everyone else took off into the woods. Suddenly, my phone lit up.

"Where are you!" Steph exclaimed, out of breath.

"The bonfire. Where are you?"

"I left. My mom came and picked me up. You have to get out now. The cops are everywhere and planning to swarm back there all at once."

"What should we do?" I asked.

At this point, I wanted to crawl into a ball and actually bawl.

"I ran across the field. Leave with our friends, and my mom and I can pick you up where she met me."

So off we went.

Step-by-step, I was making my way closer to freedom. Sprinting then tiptoeing then sprinting again, my group of friends and I made our way across the field. Beads of sweat trickled down my face. I felt like I was a criminal making a big escape.

Suddenly in the distance, a mysterious light appeared. We all dropped to the ground attempting to hide. I watched as the light slowly began to blend into the darkness (we later found out that the light was the first of many cops searching with their flashlights for kids like us hiding in the fields). The second it was gone, we took off full force. We were probably running as fast or faster than Usain Bolt to get the heck out of there. My legs didn't stop until I was safe in the truck.

Freedom. Safety. Everything was okay or so I thought.

As we made our way to town, the stress lessened, and everyone became more relaxed. I was in disbelief that we made it out alive but incredibly grateful. Approaching the first drop-off point, Liz received a text.

It read,

HELP. We're in a ditch and cops are EVERYWHERE.

A few other friends, who we did not come to the party with, had found a nearby hiding place. I felt extremely uneasy about the idea of going back, but I wasn't the driver, and it wasn't my ultimate decision. After some careful discussion, Stephanie's mom thought it was only right for us to go back and help our friends.

After dropping off the rest of the group, only Stephanie, her mother, and I remained. We cautiously made our way back to the spot where we had been picked up hours before. We could see our friends and watched as they sprinted their way toward the truck. As soon as they made their way to safety, headlights in front of us flicked on. My heart was pumping a million beats per minute as we slowly drove past the unknown vehicle.

It was a cop car. Did he see the girls crawl to safety? Why didn't the officer turn his red and blue lights on? Did he see the truck thirty minutes ago when Stephanie's mom had picked the rest of us up?

We turned right onto the next road and started on our way home. Behind us, we could see another pair of headlights, but this car was miles away. A look through the back window a few seconds later and the lights seemed much closer. The larger and clearer they became, the shakier and sweatier I started to feel. Suddenly, the red and blue started flashing. My stomach fell to the floor. I sat straight up trying to look and act as sober as possible, but I felt like all of my insides were going to explode.

"What are you doing here tonight, ma'am?" the officer sternly asked.

"I picked some of the girls up at a friend's, and I'm taking them back to my house, sir."

"You're not telling the truth," he told her.

"*Yes,* I am," she argued back.

"I watched you pick up two girls in a ditch around the corner."

My heart was beating so loudly and so fast that I thought it was going to burst out my chest. Stephanie's mom proceeded to debate, but the officer was not having it.

"Two of you in the back, get out of the car," the man swung the door open and demanded angrily. There were four girls plus Stephanie's mom in the vehicle total.

No one budged.

"Better yet, all four of you get out of the truck."

My stomach sank as deep as it possibly could (as if it could go any deeper at this point), and my back flooded with sweat. Was this really happening? Or would I wake up, and it was all a dream?

I watched as each girl took their turn getting out of the truck and walked over toward the officer. Within seconds, we were all facing him.

"You," he said, pointing to Maria who was one of the girls we picked up from the ditch, "I smell alcohol on you. Get in the car."

With a tear in her eye, she opened the door to the police car and did what was asked leaving three of us remaining. He took each of us separately and asked us questions about the events that had occurred that night. Feeling terrorized,

I tried to listen to what the other girls had said to attempt to match their stories.

"Did you drink tonight?" he firmly asked.

"Yes, officer, I did," I replied in tears.

"How much?"

"One Smirnoff." I thought lying about my intake would lessen my consequences.

"Alright, get in the car."

I did as he asked. The officer got in the driver's seat, and we drove to the entrance where the party had taken place that night. Holding hands, the three of us in the back seat (one was in the front) anxiously waited for the next move.

I had just graduated. My open house was coming up. I was registered and signed up for college classes for the fall. I had big plans to attend graduate school someday. How did this happen? Why didn't I stay back with the others? How would this affect my future?

I tried to think of any possible way to rid the taste and smell of alcohol on my breath. I swooshed my spit around, swallowed numerous times, and contemplated opening the door while the officer wasn't looking to make myself puke. Familiar underage faces were walking around followed by one or two men in uniform. Looking out the window, police cars and flashing lights seemed to stretch down the length of the whole road.

Finally, it was time to face the *real* consequences. We each got a turn to talk with the officer again. I watched as each of my friends told their story while the cop wrote in a notepad. He pulled out a Breathalyzer and each of them blew into the tiny machine. Suddenly, my door opened, and I was asked to step outside.

"I'm going to ask you to put your mouth around this device and blow as hard as you can, alright?"

"Okay," I nervously answered.

I watched as he read a digital screen on the Breathalyzer. He took me over to the front of the car and asked for my name and ID.

"Amanda Bartle. My ID is in my car. My car is not here."

Irritated, he wrote my name and asked for more personal information. I knew what he was writing. I felt incredibly humiliated and ashamed. I didn't know what I was going to tell my parents, and I did not want to find out their reaction.

He handed me my slip of paper that read "Minor in Possession" and gave me instructions on how to handle it. He told me to have a nice night and that I could leave with Stephanie's mom who had been patiently waiting for all of us. I took my time making my way back to the truck. I always thought I was too careful and too sneaky to ever get caught. But here I was with proof that anything can happen. Here I was reaping the consequences of a "fun night." Here I was questioning why I thought partying and drinking were the best way to live. Here I was speculating where I had lost myself. Here I was wondering when I had allowed these negative life choices to "soothe" my broken soul.

TRUE FULFILLMENT

I was raised in a Christian home (before the storm of divorce and after I was settled into a new routine living primarily with my mom) surrounded with godly love and sound morals and values. I was taught to love Jesus with all of my heart and soul. I was taught that too much drinking was a no-no; sex before marriage was a definite no-no, and to love unconditionally at all costs—all true things. I cannot recall a time as a child or teenager that I ever saw my parents drink more than a wine cooler, if any kind of drink at all. Essentially, I did not grow up in a home where alcohol or drugs were even remotely in the picture. Most of the things I learned about partying, I learned through friends, acquaintances, and groups that involved a mix of the two.

Besides the getting caught part, party nights were not out of the ordinary for many of my weekends. I got involved with a group of friends who lived for that lifestyle. They were sweet girls, but they enjoyed a way of life that I had never been exposed to. I am not at all blaming anyone else for my actions because they were my choices, but we are who we hang out with, right? I did not have many Christian friends. And that affected my whole high school experience.

I tried to "fit in." I wanted to "belong." I wanted to be "cool." And that was my sole focus for those four years of school. So I partied. The goal was always to drink more than I could handle. I would throw up. I would smoke. I would end up talking to boys that I knew would never fulfill what I truly valued in a man. It was about short-term satisfaction. I didn't care about tomorrow; I just wanted to forget about right now.

This way of living brought me to a dark place over time. There were nights I laid in bed holding my pillow close—tear stains on both sides for hours—wondering if there was more to life. I wrote a suicide note "just in case." I would cry hysterically in my room and wonder if physical pain would mask the emotional pain. And the interesting part is that I was a girl who had loving parents. I attended church all of my life. What went wrong? I let the echo of worldly "satisfaction" ring in my ears and take over my mind and heart. It brought me to a place so far from Jesus, and I was drowning.

Let me give you a visual. There's this path. It's a beautiful path with lots of flowers, chirping birds, and blue skies. These things make us happy, right? They make our soul feel at peace. This is the path that God has laid out for us. The more we seek Him, the more birds, flowers, and sunshine that will saturate our world. While you're on this path that we will call "the path of light," you see a separate path. We'll call this "the path of dark." And this path of dark has cupcakes, chocolate rivers, and ice cream for you to eat whenever you want (I have the biggest sweet tooth, so this is temptation for me). It's easily accessible. All you have to do is switch directions. You know that God wants to keep you on the path of light because He has the best in store, but the path of dark is so *tempting*. It's delicious. It's easy. It will make you feel "good." You think to yourself,

Well, I can just take the path of dark for a little while, and I know that the path of light will be there for me to turn back to when I'm ready. So you change directions. But you quickly realize that the path of dark is taking you deeper and further from the path of light. There are triple the number of cupcakes; the chocolate river gets larger and deeper, and gallons upon gallons of ice cream consume your journey. It tastes so good, so you keep going…and going…and going. Until one day, you take a second to evaluate your life. You are so far from the path of light; you have no idea where or how to get back to it. You feel awful from all the sugar you've been eating. You feel empty, lost, and confused.

I know this analogy seems silly, but it's a simple way to explain this process that happens to so many of us. Temptations are real and Satan is the king of temptations. In Matthew 4, he tries to tempt Jesus into turning away from God and bowing down to him. However, Jesus knows Satan's motives and tells him, "Away with you, Satan! For it is written 'You shall worship the Lord your God, and Him only you shall serve.'" Jesus recognized the devil's tricks and fled from the temptations of evil. We too need to learn to recognize the devil at work and flee from his destructive ideas.

The enemy uses temptations that make us feel good, short-term, to lure us away from God. Eventually, we are so far gone that we have no idea how to get back on the path that we know in our heart of hearts is the right one for us. We feel disappointed, ashamed, and unworthy to turn back to our Christian values. So what do we do? Or what did I do? I kept right on the path of dark hoping that something good would come of it. I felt like too much of a disappointment to even talk with God. Why would He want anything to do with a sinner like me?

By doing this, *I was giving the enemy what he wanted.* His whole goal is to keep us away from Jesus. If he can get into our heads and hold us hostage in guilt, disappointment, and failure, we are really giving Satan the trophy.

We live in a culture that tells us the key to fun is to have sex with multiple people, drink then drink some more, and whatever else your instant "fulfillment" might be. We are a "goody-two-shoes" if we *don't* do these things. We aren't *really* living. Our society tells us these are a few pieces of the satisfying life puzzle. In high school, I felt like I had to conform to this identity to be "worthy," have friends, and have the "time of my life."

But worthy for who? Who was I living for? Who was I trying to please? It certainly wasn't my Creator. I was stuck. I was lost trying to fill a void that I would never be able to on my own.

And don't take me wrong, I'm not against alcohol. But the main idea here with this example is the difference between doing something because you are trying to drown out your problems by abusing it to fill a hole in your heart compared to occasionally enjoying something knowing your heart is in a good place.

The key word is *fulfillment*. Where are you seeking it, and how does the "thing" you are trying to use to fulfill make you feel? Are you like I was trying to fill a hole with instant gratification? This feels good at the time but leads to long-term destruction and emptiness. I thought the rush of adrenaline that came from the "fun" I was having would last forever until I was alone in my thoughts and wondered where in the world my heart was. I longed for peace in my soul. How did I trail so far off the perfect path of light that Jesus intended for me to stay on?

What happened to being admired for having a burning passion in our souls to serve Jesus? What happened to *that* being the key to living a satisfying life? How did our world get so turned upside down that the individuals who love Jesus and want to live out His purpose have to face worldly rejection? Or why do those who have a curious soul about this Christian life they've heard of feel as if they cannot dive deeper because society tells them it's not "fun" to live that way?

Where are you seeking fulfillment?

Where are you seeking fulfillment? Are you getting drunk every weekend in hopes that the adventurous night you might experience will fill that void? Are you sleeping with anyone searching for a feeling of worth? Are you gambling your life away because you think money will make you happy? Are you spending money left and right because you think having all these things will somehow give you the peace you long for?

> Blessed are those who hunger and thirst
> for righteousness, for they shall be filled.
> (Matthew 5:6)

Jesus is the answer. He is the *only* way to true whole-hearted fulfillment. And the best part is regardless of where you are in your spiritual journey, He *wants* to know you. I cannot stress this enough. I used to think that I was too far "gone" to ever be able to talk to God again. I used to think I was not worthy of his attention. But how incredibly wrong I was. Do not let the enemy use your past or recent mistakes to make you think you're not worthy to come back to Jesus. He welcomes you *just as you are.*

> You will seek me and find me, when you seek me with all of your heart. (Jeremiah 29:13)

Jesus is the way, the truth, and the life for a heart of fulfillment..

He is an amazing healer and can transform your sins to be used for His mighty good. Your life was never intended to feel broken and alone. Lay your sins at the cross and humbly give Him your whole heart. I promise that you will experience a kind of fullness you have never felt before. You *are* worthy. You *are* His child. You *are* a part of a beautiful plan. He *does* want to give you a life drenched in fulfillment. Seek Him during the best of the best. Seek Him during the lowest of lows. Flee from earthly satisfaction, for that is the enemy pulling you into a lonely trap. Jesus is the way, the truth, and the life for a heart of fulfillment. Will you let Him satisfy that void?

CHAPTER 3

Healthy Means "Put Together"

THE WRONG REASON

I have always loved living a healthy lifestyle. When I was in high school, I played volleyball, and I also liked to run during the summertime. Since I graduated high school, exercising and eating good food have been my outlet, my "thing" if you will. Give me a gym, an open road, a full kitchen, and I work with what I have to get a workout in or cook myself a healthy meal.

I am passionate about healthy living (a.k.a. balanced living) and love to live it to the best of my ability every single day. It really is a great thing and obviously has so many benefits. So please take me honestly and seriously when I say I would never discourage exercise or eating well.

What I *am* going to challenge from my own experience is your why. Why do you eat well and exercise? Or why don't you? Seriously think about that question.

For me, for a long time, it was about appearance. Being healthy and fit meant that "I had my life together." And what I really was after was the way that healthy habits made my body look.

Let me stop right there and explain that I'm not at all saying it's wrong to want your body to physically look better by developing healthy behaviors. Feeling confident in your own skin is so important, and I'm not discouraging that. Heck, I geek out when I notice small improvements in my body, and I hope you do too. The place I'm going with this is where is your heart at? What is the real motive behind why you're making these lifestyle changes?

Let me dig even deeper. Are you going to the gym to fill a void in hopes that looking fit will make you feel whole?

When I graduated high school and started college, I was completely and utterly lost. I lived alone in my studio apartment and only had a couple of friends at the community college I was attending. I felt confused about what my future held. I had been coping with a breakup for quite a while, and living alone and having a lot of time to think did not always bring me to a happy place mentally. My relationship with God was not a healthy one. I was an immature eighteen-year-old who was lost on so many levels.

So I got a gym membership. I decided to release some of that negative energy in a positive way. I became intrigued with healthy living and devoted a lot of time to bettering myself. This in itself was great. I am so thankful that I was able to channel my confusion into developing beneficial habits that are instilled in me at this point in my life. That was an extremely positive thing.

The negative thing was that I became anxiously addicted to it. I felt irritable if I couldn't get a workout in because I had this false conception that missing days meant that I would gain weight. If I had class and had to work, I would go to the gym anywhere between 11:00 p.m.–2:00 a.m. because missing a workout meant I wasn't "fit" enough or "dedicated" enough. Every single workout *had* to include a two-to-three-mile run. No excuses.

I would beat myself up over eating bad food. And when I say *beat myself up*, I mean I would get so deep into a negative space in my head over eating a brownie that I would end up in tears. I would feel this tremendous amount of guilt going to parties knowing that I was going to binge and "destroy" all of my progress. I would log every single food that I ate that day and estimate the amount of calories that I had consumed through this app that would tell me how many calories I needed to burn in order to lose weight. I weighed a lot of my food to make sure I could account for every single calorie.

"Healthy" to me meant working out for a minimum of one hour *every single day* and eating nothing but veggies and chicken *every single day*. And I don't think there has been a single week where I have ever achieved that. The insane expectation to live a "perfectly healthy" life became an obsession. I could never live up to my expectations, and it started to really take a toll on my mental health. I was never "good enough" because I set this outrageous goal that was not at all attainable for me, and I was extremely hard on myself for it. I was on the right track creating lifestyle changes, but my obsession to look the way social media portrays a "fit girl" was killing me emotionally and mentally.

Hear me out. I'm not saying it's not awesome to be dedicated. I'm not saying if you do those things, you're bad or over the top. A lot of those things can be super helpful tools to lose weight when you want or need to. And if you are the kind of person who can live that strict lifestyle and are completely happy and satisfied with it, I am so happy for you. That is great, and please keep up the good work, and post tips on how you do it so the rest of us can learn from you. Seriously! My story, however, is that I made myself miserable trying to keep up with the rigid rules I set. I was 125 pounds and eighteen years old giving myself these guidelines that my body didn't need. I could never ever meet the minimum requirements, and I was constantly putting myself down for it.

The lifestyle I was creating might have been an "outlet," but it was also a distraction from facing an emptiness in my heart and trying to fulfill a false worldly image that I would never be able to live up to. I found myself trying to eat a certain way and workout with these high expectations in order to "fulfill" not only myself but also a distorted cultural view that focuses heavily on physical appearance. I was putting my focus on my body to avoid the other "stuff" going on in my heart. I cared more about trying to make sure the world saw me as this fit and perfect girl rather than addressing the spiritual issues that I was trying to hide.

THE RIGHT REASON

The funny thing is that even though I tried so hard to live this perfectly healthy life, I never looked like the fit girls on Instagram…and I never will. My body was created to look a certain way, and no matter how hard I try, there are certain characteristics that I will never be able to change. This is true for all of us.

Did my body look better then than it does today? Heck yes, however, the way I view a healthy lifestyle now is much different than it was back then. I enjoy life more than I used to. I probably will always struggle with body image to some degree because I always have been hard on myself, and it's easy to fall back into bad habits, but overall, my "healthy lifestyle" expectations are completely different than they were when I was a freshman in college.

I value other areas of my well-being that I never put too much effort into before. I try to sleep more, take care of my mental health, and give myself time to simply enjoy life. Some days, I sleep more and skip working out. *And that's okay.* Some days, I eat ice cream for dinner because I'm craving sweets. *And that's okay.* Some days, I take time to unwind and take care of myself mentally. *And that's okay.* Life was meant for balance and to be enjoyed.

I now aim to eat relatively clean most days. I try to resist sweets as much as I can. I try to do a structured workout or at least some kind of exercise most days (even if it's not as intense as I used to think it needed to be). I give myself room to mess up and do my best not to sweat the small stuff. Every phase of life is different, and I try to adjust my expectations accordingly. And the best part is that if I totally blow all those goals during one particular week, I remind myself that there are fifty-one other weeks in the year, and all I can do is my best.

I encourage you, if you don't prioritize your health right now, work at it. Maybe my lifestyle expectations don't work for your life, whether they're too much or too little. The awesome thing is it's your life, so you can set whatever expectations you freaking want that work for you.

God even calls us to care about our bodies and our health.

> Or do you not know that your body is the temple of the Holy Spirit who is in you, whom you have from God, and you are not your own? For you were bought at a price; therefore, glorify God in your body and in your spirit, which are God's. (1 Corinthians 6:19–20)

God commands us to take care of our bodies because they are a gift from Him. Exercising, fueling our bodies with nutritious food, and self-care in general keep our minds clear and focused. If we keep our physical bodies healthy, our minds will follow, and we can more effectively

If we keep our physical bodies healthy, our minds will follow, and we can more effectively fix our eyes on Jesus and the will He has for our lives.

fix our eyes on Jesus and the will He has for our lives. We cannot effectively fill someone else's cup or fulfill God's will if we are not filling our own first. Part of this involves taking the time to take care of yourself.

The biggest tip I have to effectively do so is to *give yourself grace.* Life is literally insane sometimes, and you're not going to get it right every week. Make mental notes of your effort and every victory, big or small, and hang onto those. Give yourself a mental trophy for going on a thirty-minute walk today. Pat yourself on the back because you squeezed in one healthy meal today. Be proud of yourself because you chose the salad over the burger on your date today. Be proud of every healthy choice no matter how *big* or *small*. Because every one of those choices is a baby step toward living a healthier life overall. And *that* is worth celebrating.

So I've given some advice on the execution of a healthy lifestyle, but what about all the deep emptiness stuff in our hearts I was talking about earlier? This is where we get to talk about that part.

Like I said before, when I was living this rigorous lifestyle as a freshman in college before I had adopted the way I live now, what I was really doing was avoiding a hole in my heart by chasing after what the world told me would make me happy. Surprise, surprise, I was chasing after a fulfillment that did not exist. I thought the appearance of healthy living and a fit body would make me feel whole. But obviously, it didn't.

> For bodily exercise profits a little, but godliness is profitable for all things, having promises of the life that now is and of that which is to come. (1 Timothy 4:8)

I just told you to try to prioritize eating better and to exercise when you can, and now I'm showing you a verse that says "exercise profits a little." Trust me; I'm aware of this. And I am also aware that "bodily exercise" can be interpreted in so many ways, but for the purpose of this chapter I am taking it literally. Hang tight.

The ultimate message I'm trying to send here is yes, make your health a priority. However, that is not the most important thing you should do with your life. Exercise is good. Eating well is good. Taking care of yourself is good. But if your healthy lifestyle is driving you to push God out of the picture, there's a problem. And that was my problem.

Without being in the right place with God, every other aspect of your life will feel off, empty, or inadequate.

My philosophy was "exercise profits a lot, and godliness profits when I have time for it." I cared more about giving my attention and energy to satisfy a worldly attraction rather than making God my number one priority. Spiritual health is the most important part of your well-being. Without being in the right place with God, every other aspect of your life will feel off, empty, or inadequate.

I challenge you to look at your motives and get in touch with the truth of your heart. Are you nurturing your soul with the Word of God on a regular basis? Or are your meal prep and workouts more important? Are you striving for a healthy life because you know deep down there's a hurt in your heart that you're trying to distract yourself from? Or are you on the flip side and don't put the energy into taking care of yourself, but you know it's important and ultimately a call from God?

Whichever side you're on, know that God sees you, and He hears you. He knows if your heart is aching for His love, and He simply wants you to take the time to come home to Him and to stop making excuses. He sees the desire you have to take care of the body He gave you—mentally and/or physically—and wants you to come to Him in humility and prayer and ask for the energy, strength, and/or time to be revealed to you so you can make yourself a priority.

Healthy living is important, but God is most important.

A healthy soul and a healthy relationship with God go hand in hand with maintaining a healthy lifestyle. However, remember that "godliness is profitable for *all* things, but exercise profits a little." Healthy living is important, but God is *most* important.

CHAPTER 4

You Will Never Be Good Enough

HOW I THOUGHT I WAS DEFINED

In fourth grade, all that mattered was who was hosting the next sleepover. I never worried about what clothes I was wearing (they were probably cousin hand-me-downs). My hair was always done however it naturally fell with a good morning brush. All I knew about makeup was that my mom wore it. I didn't have a clue about shaving my legs, and I didn't care. I made friends based on personality and who was the most fun to be around. Outer appearance was not a concern in the slightest bit.

Fifth grade came around, and my world was rocked. I had just started a new school. I have always been a little more introverted when I meet people initially (I think so anyway), so it was way out of my comfort zone to talk to new people and make new friends. Everyone knew each other, and I was the lost duckling. In addition to feeling totally uncomfortable around unfamiliar faces, kids started to talk about things that had never mattered much to me. Clothing brands were, all of a sudden, a huge deal. Kids were starting to hit their growth spurts, so now height was starting to become something that everyone was judged by. I was the new short weirdo who wore a Walmart Pooh Bear hoodie that was three times too big for me on the first day.

First, height and clothes, second, makeup and hairstyles—these were the next "important things" once sixth grade began. Dark black eyeliner and pin straight hair was the "thing." Bless my grandma's soul for always telling me how cute my natural hair was. It took a long time for that hair to rejuvenate the wavy curls I destroyed through years of torching them with a flat iron. It was difficult to "be cool" if you didn't keep up with these appearances. Being popular mattered to me at this age. So whether I *really* liked the way it looked or not, I fried my hair and caked on the eyeliner anyway.

Seventh grade, *ohhhhhh,* seventh grade—this was a big year for a girl. Puberty was causing my body to put on weight and look curvier. I was eagerly waiting to start my period because that meant I was finally a "real woman." Boys were starting to interest me, and I noticed boys were becoming more interested *in* me. This is the real year that appearances, self-worth, and how I believed I was defined really came into play.

My mom is from Chile. If geography isn't your strong suit, I'll tell you that Chile is a country in South America. So naturally, I have dark hair. And with that dark hair comes unwanted hair on my face. I was born with peach fuzz above my lip and small dark hairs on my chin. Were they noticeable? Probably not. But when a couple of boys started to make fun of me, they were the only things I saw when I looked in the mirror. I was thirteen years old and extremely self-conscious of my "mustache" and "beard."

I started waxing. Is waxing those areas an issue? No. But the fact that I was only thirteen and obsessing over small, hardly noticeable body hair *was* an issue.

And it didn't stop there. Eighth grade came around, and I started getting laughed at for my "bushy eyebrows." They weren't even bushy. Women today would kill for the full beautiful brows I had in middle school. But I was thoroughly convinced they were disgustingly ugly, so to the mirror with tweezers I went.

Lip/chin hair, bushy eyebrows, and then came the acne. Like many thirteen-year-olds, my face started to break out. I never had severe acne, but I thought the world was ending every time a few pimples would pop up. I cared about how others saw my skin. I cared about having a perfect complexion. I would try these "at-home remedies" that perhaps do work if you don't do them fifty times in a row expecting the pimples to instantly disappear. My skin would get more irritated, and so would I.

Last but not least of the middle school insecurities was the dreaded number on the scale. I was obsessed with it. If someone would have told me how much that does not matter in middle school, I wouldn't have cared. I still would have watched the scale like a hawk and stressed about any increase in the number.

In conclusion, I was stressed and anxious over my body image.

At this point in my life, I was getting ready to enter the ninth grade. As you can see, what mattered to me had everything to do with how others viewed me. My clothes, my hair, my makeup, my eyebrows, my facial hair, my weight, and my skin were major priorities for me. I was about to enter high school where my competence with these things would determine my place on the social hierarchy of coolness. And the bottom of that hierarchy was not a place I wanted to be.

One of the biggest concerns for me as a freshman in high school was how the boys saw me. Did they think I was popular enough? Did they think I was pretty enough? Did they think I dressed well enough? I remember these questions haunting my brain as I entered the realm of older boys. Their opinions mattered. I wanted to be noticed. I wanted to be "loved." And to gain that attention, I focused massively on my appearance.

The same ole desire for boys to notice me and classmates to respect me as a "cool kid" continued into tenth grade. However, a huge important appearance factor arose during that particular year. A specific something became a huge deal, and that something was pretty pathetic: jeans. Let me say that again—jeans. The prices of the brand that everyone obsessed over ranged anywhere from $80–$200. You might think this is completely stupid, and I agree, but it was sincerely a huge deal in my small town. They were on everyone's Christmas list. The more you had, the more popular you were. If you wore them in public, people knew you were a "somebody."

The reason I'm specifically mentioning *jeans* is to give an example of the way my brain prioritized appearances at that point in my life. I was an extremely materialistic sixteen-year-old who was overly concerned with what I wore and where that placed me on the popularity pyramid. I wanted to be known, and designer jeans were the key.

I was seventeen going on eighteen and incredibly confused about what *really* mattered. My priority was making sure I looked "cool" to everyone else, and I never felt like enough. For years, I had grown up being told by society that I was defined by my appearance, and now I was months away from graduating high school and I was about to be exposed to the real world feeling empty, unworthy, and constantly struggling to see my value.

HOW I AM ACTUALLY DEFINED

"My skin could be clearer…"
"I could lose a few pounds…"
"My hair color is ugly…"
"I wish I was taller…"
"If only my eyes were a different color…"
"Is there a way to change my voice?"
"My teeth suck…"

Sound familiar? Throughout my teenage years, these statements and more haunted me. I never understood how my worth was measured. I was on a mission to please the world and "keep up with the Joneses." I let my physical appearance define what was important about me, and I found myself constantly disappointed.

Where did these ideas of how my worth was defined come from? Without a doubt, comparison is the culprit. As little girls, we laugh a lot; we play with anyone and everyone, and we live in the moment. As we grow older, we are exposed to the worldly image of what the "ideal woman" looks like. We exchange the innocent joy we once thrived off for the search to be perfect according to society. We want our waists to be tiny and our skin to be flawless. We see edited photos and feel instantly unworthy and bad about ourselves because we don't look that way. We focus so much on physical appearance and think that if we just look a certain way, we will feel like enough.

I think the saddest part is the transition from innocence to comparison. When do girls exchange that free-spirited love for one another for body image-destroying comparison? Who said that it matters what we look like? Who decided that it was important for women to strive for "perfection?" We get stuck in this mindset of trying to look flawless so we're "worth something." We subconsciously think that looking perfect from the outside will determine our value and will bring us the love we long for. It's a sick cycle that so many of us, including myself, get stuck in. When we don't measure up to the "ideal image" of a woman, we feel failure, depression, and worthlessness.

I think many of us fail to realize that this is the enemy hard at work. He wants us to feel horrible about ourselves. He craves for us to compare and nitpick our imperfections. He wants us to determine our worth based on what society views as "perfect." His goal is to make us feel unloved. He thrives off our tears, aching hearts, and constant struggle to look and act "pretty." He wants us to feel our lowest of lows every day so we turn away from the one who wants the total opposite for us.

The enemy can put negative self-thoughts in our heads. He can expose us to the media and Hollywood's idea of what a woman "should" look like to make us compare. He can attack our hearts and do his best to make us feel like we aren't good enough. He has a lot of power to make us think extremely negatively about ourselves. He uses society's views to his advantage to affect the way we determine our worth.

But one thing the devil cannot do is take away the fact that we were created by someone who loves us unconditionally, flaws and all. We were put on this earth with our imperfections because we were never supposed to be judged by them. We were created perfectly and uniquely by God's hands. The flaws we so harshly evaluate ourselves by were not mistakes. God made us perfect just the way we are. We were made to care about our hearts and how we're fulfilling our godly purpose through spreading God's unfailing love to the world around us. But instead, we live in a culture where we have become so obsessed with our faults and appearances that we fail to see the beauties and gifts God has blessed us with.

You might be thinking, *Why would God give us imperfections if He didn't want us to focus on them?* Well, I don't have the direct answer to that question, but I do know His purpose was never for us to obsess over them. Our world has made the negative things about ourselves the center of our attention. There's a product for everything. Commercials are filled with emphasizing our problems and how they can give us the "solution." Self-love is hardly encouraged. We grow up focusing on the things we want to change about ourselves but never take the time to explore and appreciate the beautiful pieces.

We forget that there is so much to love about who we are and that God gave us gifts to utilize, not to shove under the rug so we can keep feeling sorry about our "deficiencies." We were put here the way we are for a reason. Maybe you struggle with your weight, but you fail to see the generous heart that God gave you. Maybe you were born with a birth or physical defect, but your independence is an admirable gift from God. Or maybe you just beat yourself up over so many physical things about you, but God sees a beautiful soul with so many talents that are waiting to be recognized and used. We fail to see that the small flaw means absolutely nothing compared to the purpose that God put us here for. We are caught up in trying to satisfy the world, not Jesus. Whatever your negative thing or things might be, just know that they were not meant to be dwelled upon but meant to be overcome and used in a good way for His glory.

You are enough just the way you are.

You are enough just the way you are. The only opinion that should matter is God's. His approval is the only one you should be seeking. Your heart matters—your looks do not.

> So God created man in his own image, in the image of God he created Him; male and female he created them. (Genesis 1:27)

Your heart matters— your looks do not.

We were created in His image, not society's. Everything about us has been carefully thought out and designed a certain way. When we see ourselves poorly, our Father weeps because He sees our beauty and defines us by so much more than what we look like. It's time for us to view ourselves the way that Jesus does with grace, love, and mercy and seek the gifts and the godly potential that He craves for us to pursue.

> Why do you beautify your way to seek love? (Jeremiah 2:33).

In other words, why do we try so hard to change ourselves and conform to society's view of "beautiful" to seek self-worth through the world's approval? We always have been and always will be enough for Jesus just the way we are. He knows we aren't perfect. He knows we make sinful mistakes. He knows some days we can't help but focus on the negatives about ourselves. That's why He gives us grace. However, He wants us to actively seek our worth through His eyes so we understand what it means to *truly* feel that we are enough. He desires our whole hearts and wants us to come to Him with our self-doubt so He can show us how we are worth an eternity more than what the world says we are. He wants us to trust Him with our hearts so he can show us what real love feels like. He longs for us to pursue Him and seek His will to find a fulfilling joy that this world cannot offer. We are already perfect to Him with all our imperfections. His value is all that really matters, and it has nothing to do with the critical thoughts we have about ourselves. It has everything to do with our hearts, our purpose, and how we love one another.

We are already perfect to Him with all our imperfections.

Will you let Him show you your real worth?

CHAPTER 5

Money and Titles Matter

THE KEYS TO HAPPINESS

What do you want to be when you grow up?

What are you going to do with that degree?

What is your next career step?

These were and always have been some of my least favorite questions to get asked. The looks of disappointment when it was obvious that I was not confident in my answer were always extremely frustrating. As a college kid with a degree that is typically only used to further one's education, a "stepping-stone degree" if you will, these questions came up A LOT. And my answer was *constantly* changing.

I always wanted to be something big. I wanted an important career that made lots of money and was admirable in the eyes of society. At my high school graduation open house, I told people I wanted to go into health care to "probably be a doctor, a cardiologist to be specific." Little did I know how easy it was to say that as a high school graduate until college chemistry came into my life. I quickly realized that a premed degree and my chemistry grades were not going to be friends. So I sought out other health care jobs. I shadowed physical therapy and occupational therapy. Something felt off about both of those, so I looked into becoming a physician assistant. I spent a semester shadowing one, and once again, something just didn't sit right with me (and chemistry was also a must for this one which meant probably a no for me).

It was not that I entirely disliked those careers. They all had their pros and cons, but something just didn't feel right for me doing those jobs for forty hours per week, every single week. Some might say, "Well, all jobs have the things you don't like that you just do anyway." I agree with that, but what I felt was a different kind of uncertainty. If I was going to spend the time and money on furthering my education, I wanted to make sure it was 100 percent for me. I wanted to make sure it was my *purpose*, not just a job. The amount of hesitation I had while shadowing those careers was enough for me to withdraw from pursuing them. I had always been extremely sure about going to graduate school, but I was running out of options.

One day, I can't remember how this came about, but there was a girl I had known through mutual friends that also attended my university. We got coffee and talked about career stuff. She had the same degree path as mine and had always planned to go to graduate school for occupational therapy. She was a go-getter, like me, and had many hours of experience under her belt much earlier than many of our colleagues. We both talked about the career itself and how we both weren't sure if it was really for us. She told me that she had made the bold decision to leave the idea of occupational therapy behind to pursue a career with her exercise science degree.

A gleam of hope is what that was for me. Whatever I decided at the time or in the future, I was going to be okay. Whether I pursued something with solely my bachelor's degree or decided to continue my education after graduation, I wasn't alone in the uncertainty.

Time went by, and I had been in a constant battle with myself between trying to figure out which graduate program was right for me or whether I should continue my education after obtaining my four-year degree at all. A friend sent me a screenshot of something that a former medical student posted on Instagram that completely changed my mindset. Lucky for you, I found the exact caption that this student had posted. Be prepared to be mind-blown.

> Big announcement: I did not return for my second year, second semester of medical school. I have been putting off making this announcement for several weeks because I did not know how I wanted to go about telling this to you all. I have spoken to friends and family regarding the situation, and if you are close to me and just

now hearing this for the first time, I apologize that I did not tell you before posting this. This was obviously a tough decision for me and something that I have thought about deeply for several months prior to making the choice to remove myself from school. So why did I make this decision? Growing up, I had always thought that being a physician was my calling and what I was destined to become. I have several family members who are physicians and thought that this was what I should do with my life as well. After the first year of medical school I started to question why I was passionate about practicing medicine. I couldn't come up with an answer that satisfied myself, so I shadowed to see if I could find the answer there. This is something that I wish I had done earlier and to a deeper extent because it would have saved me a lot of time (and money) discovering that this was in fact not something that I was passionate about and definitely something that I did not want to spend the rest of my life doing. I tried toughing it out a little longer (this past semester) to see if my mind would change, but it did not. I am confident in my decision to leave medical school and excited to pursue other endeavors that I am passionate about. I apologize if I let anyone down, but I want you all to know that if you feel stuck or discouraged with your current situation really evaluate where you are at and if you have felt you need to make a change, DO IT. Make sure that you are not acting out of impulse first though…

Pretty crazy stuff, huh? It goes to show the importance of truly *loving* what you're doing because your job is what you will do for the rest of your life. If you don't have a passion for it, then it probably isn't for you. And that is where I found myself super confused. I wanted so badly to *want* to do those careers, but nothing was clicking. It was an uneasy feeling for a girl who plans like crazy and had always had in her head that she was going to pursue years of education to, all of a sudden, not have a solid postgraduate plan.

What took me a really long time to realize is what my intentions *actually* were with me choosing one of those professional careers. I was looking for (1) job security, (2) credentials, and (3) a big paycheck. I wanted to know for sure I would be able to find a job after I graduated. I wanted the letters behind my name to make myself feel important. And I wanted to know that I would be making enough money so I could buy everything and anything that I wanted. Sadly, our world (or at least our culture) revolves around these three things in many scenarios. These three things that we constantly chase after and find that they don't hold as much value as we think. These three things that God tells us do not matter compared to what He really has in store for our lives. These three things that God was wrestling my heart for while I was trying to choose my future.

THE REAL JOY

Let me preface this chapter by saying that every career that I mentioned is a GREAT career. We need those people who have the passion to do them to keep us healthy. And for all I know, maybe God will call me to pursue one of them someday. The point I'm trying to make is that we all have passions, desires, and gifts that God has blessed us with, and it is essential that we use those in whatever way God calls us to in whatever His timing might be for true fulfillment. I personally was chasing those career paths for the wrong reasons at the wrong time and that is why I believe they didn't feel right for me.

What kind of "success" was I chasing by shadowing these careers and not really digging deep into my heart to ask myself if I was passionate about them? Earthly accomplishment. I was so focused on trying to do something that would make people think highly of me that I was completely shutting off the passion searching piece of my heart. I should have been asking myself what was important in the eyes of God, what gifts I was given, and how I could potentially mesh these things into a career or find a different way to pursue my God-given talents. I should have been seeking Jesus's success.

I was told from a young age that the medical field was a good one for girls to go into. I never gave myself the opportunity to search other areas because I wanted to make everyone else happy with my career choice. So I stuck to that and found myself lost.

Why didn't these job options feel right for me? Everyone has a calling. I firmly believe we all have a place that is exactly where we are supposed to be in each phase of our lives. Because those careers were not my calling either for that specific time of my life or at all; I found myself in a very sad and confused place. I was chasing after the wrong things. I wasn't focused on God's plan, but I was focused on my own earthly timing and desires and what job I could do that would give me the most money, material things, and an easy job search. But God doesn't care about those things. He has a special place for each of us at every moment of our lives where we are needed the most. And the most satisfying job you or I will ever do is the one that God places on our hearts for us to do and opens doors for. That uneasiness I felt while shadowing, I believe, was put on my heart for a reason. I was seeking these jobs for the wrong purposes. I was trying to force careers into my life on my own time and not allowing God to carve my path according to His desires using the passions He has placed on my heart.

Maybe you're reading this, and you're thinking you can't relate because college wasn't your thing, and you went straight into the workforce. Or maybe you're a mom and college or work just has not been feasible for you. Well, guess what? This chapter is still applicable to you. We all have confusion and concern for the unknown future. I had "plans," and what I mean by that is I thought I knew what I wanted until I really dug deep into my heart and started to think about what gave me purpose. And the very thing that has been giving me purpose is pursuing the will of God and trusting in His plan while tossing mine aside. And why do this? Because God knows what's *best* for us. We might think we do, but He knows our hearts better than anyone, and He put you here to do something special that only you can do that will bring you a fulfillment you never would have experienced if you followed your own ideas. You have plans too. We all do. But I encourage you to dig a little deeper into your heart and ask yourself what really lights that fire inside your soul. How can you use that to not only bring yourself joy but bring glory to God's kingdom? Bringing glory to God's kingdom should be your first priority.

To make this a little simpler, what I am trying to say is don't chase a job or a dream or a future for the wrong reasons, and keep your mind and heart wide open. Pray about your future and where God wants to use you and lead you. You might be like me and have always "thought" you wanted to do one thing, but you're feeling a pull to do something completely different. And if that's the case, *chase it.* Do not let the world's idea of success hold you back from doing what God has laid on your heart to do. He will take care of you and give you everything you need, including the ultimate fulfillment, if you follow the plan He's calling you to follow. Pray for the doors to open and jump right in.

At the end of my four-year degree, I had no idea what I was doing. I had prayed for months for God to reveal the next steps for me. I faithfully waited (with a lot of tears and frustration) until God made it extremely obvious which door I was supposed to go through next. I don't entirely understand why He wanted me to enter that door, but that is not for me to know. My job is to pursue it with my whole heart and trust that God will lead me toward the next path when the time is right.

God will provide all the money that I need. He will reveal where I need to go during each phase of my life. He will open the right doors for me in His timing, not my own. I personally just have to realize that the letters behind my name do not define who I am. What really matters is what we do with our time here on earth to give God the glory and to love people deeply. The credentials mean nothing in heaven if that is not my calling and I am not fulfilling my special purpose.

Think about the almost doctor who dropped out of medical school to chase after passions that he never knew he had until he really thought about his reasons for pursuing medical school. If you're in a similar place in your life whether it be in college, the job you're currently doing, or whatever else you're putting your time and effort into right now, ask yourself what your "why" is. Does it fulfill a desire in your heart? Does it bring you such joy that you just know that is the place you're supposed to be? Do you feel like you're using your gifts to fulfill your godly purpose? If your answer is no to any of these questions, it might be time to reevaluate what you're doing and why you're doing it. Do you believe where you are is where God wants you to be? Do you believe it is a part of His plan? Or are you there for selfish reasons like a big paycheck or the credentials that make you feel "worthy?"

We all have God-given talents, abilities, and spiritual gifts. We might not be meant to use any or all of these in our career, but you sure as heck should be loving what you do and know that it is where you're meant to be. God places desires, passions, and goals in our hearts for a reason. Your job should reflect fulfillment in at least some of these areas of your heart to feel the utmost joy in what you do. And if your job does not bring fulfillment, then you should be seeking to glorify God in whatever ways you possibly can in the position that you're in. That will bring joy and purpose to your life as well. Ask for guidance along your journey through life so you can be fulfilling a beautiful uniquely designed plan that has your very best in mind.

What happens when you ask for guidance and you get led to a place you never thought you would be? Trust. All you can do is know that God's plans are bigger than your own and that you are in the position that you are in for a reason. You have no idea whose prayers He might be answering through you. You have to believe with all that you have that He has it all under control and is working everything out for your good because He loves you more than you can imagine. But man oh man, trusting is so much easier said than done sometimes.

You also have to remember that each step in life might not be your favorite step. It could be a stepping-stone intended to shape and grow you in ways you don't understand to prepare you for the next place that God wants to take you. It could be a period of waiting and testing. God wants us to put our full faith and trust in Him, and sometimes He wants us to be patient and trust that He still has everything under control despite His silence.

It's hard. It's hard to know where and what God wants us to do. It's hard to trust that we're following His plan and doing what He wants us to do. It's hard to sacrifice our own earthly desires to do what God placed us here to do. It's especially hard to do this when all of society around us screams the importance of "worldly success," a.k.a. job, financial status, and security.

If we truly want whole happiness, a full heart of joy, and career satisfaction at its greatest, we have to let go of these things the world tells us matter in our career and seek "Jesus's success." We need to find our gifts and utilize them in ways that bring God the glory, serve and love people, and fill a void in our hearts knowing that this is our calling. We have to trust that God will provide the financial stability that we need and will lead us into the position that we're meant to be in.

> The Lord says, "I will guide you along the
> best pathway for your life. I will advise
> you and watch over you." (Psalm 32:8)

We have to believe and trust this promise with all our hearts. We have to know that He loves us so much that He

We need to find our gifts and utilize them in ways that bring God the glory, serve and love people, and fill a void in our hearts knowing that this is our calling.

has created a future just for us. We have to forget what the world says is important and seek God's ways.

What is your why? Do you feel as if you're pursuing Jesus's plan for your life? Or are you barely getting by and feeling unhappy, unsatisfied, and lost wondering what your purpose is?

Make your biggest goal on earth be to glorify God in *all* things. Pray about what you were *made* to do; *find* that calling, and *do it well*. Here's a prayer that my mama prayed when she was in nursing

Make your biggest goal on earth be to glorify God in all things.

school and passed it on to me. This is my go-to when I'm feeling anxious, sad, or confused about not knowing my next step. I encourage you to pray this too if you're

struggling like I have at some points in my life. Submit yourself, your heart, and your work to the Lord, and I promise you He will be faithful (in His timing) in guiding you in the direction that He wants you to go—a place that you were meant for all along.

Lord, open the doors where you want me to go, and close the doors that are not meant for me. Make it *crystal clear* for me so I know I'm doing exactly Your will. My purpose is to serve You in my work, and I pray that You reveal to me where You need me the most and where I will bring You the most glory. Amen.

CHAPTER 6

You Can't Afford to Give

THE CONVICTION

My favorite day of the week is Sunday. I love to get dolled up, go to church, maybe get brunch afterward, and enjoy the rest of the relaxing day. A sunny, warm Sunday where I can spend time outside is like icing on the cake. There's a different feel to that particular day of the week. I wake up in a good mood. I feel full of humility. Sundays just make me want to be a good person and spread all the love in my heart. God's day is my favorite day.

I was sitting in church one morning feeling exactly how I just described. It was a hands-in-the-air kind of worship day. My heart was feeling so full of joy and Jesus. It was November, so Christmas was shortly approaching.

The sermon had been great; my coffee was delicious, and the sun was shining brighter than ever. The pastor had said something about these Christmas trees that were sit-

73

ting in the lobby with paper ornaments that had the gender and age of kids who lived in the community whose families could not afford Christmas presents for them. He asked that we pray about these children, and if our hearts felt led to provide presents for one, two, or three of them this Christmas, then to feel free to choose an age and gender that best fit us.

Usually, whenever the pastor would talk about giving in *any* way, shape, or form, I would automatically tune out because I was a college kid, and I assumed everyone understood the income of a student. Tithing, donations, food drives, you name it, and I acted like I wasn't even a part of the audience because, in all reality, feeding myself some weeks meant pinching pennies. I naturally do have a giving heart and it fills me with so much joy to be able to act on that part of who I am. But being on a tight budget I did not put too much thought into giving to someone I didn't even know when I had bills to pay and my own mouth to feed.

On this particular day, something hit me right in the conviction corner of my soul. I sat in my chair, and my heart felt heavy for those kids. I thought to myself, *There is no way I could afford a gift for someone else when I can barely afford any for my family right now.* And then I felt a tug at my heart and a soft whisper.

How can you not sacrifice some money that you would probably spend on yourself to give to one of my children when I have always provided you with more than you need?

Ouch. The truth of the matter is God was right. I had been extremely blessed to have my amazing parents help me with many college expenses. My tuition had been paid for by hard work, scholarships, and random grants that came out of nowhere (literally). Some weeks were harder than others, and every college kid I know lives paycheck to paycheck spending their money on groceries, utilities, emergency coffee, etc. In a nutshell, I graduated with a bachelor's degree completely debt-free, literally by the grace of God, and I couldn't find it in my budget to sacrifice an extra twenty dollars when I have had everything and more provided for me?

I walked out of church that day with an ornament that read, "Girl, 13 years old." I had one hundred dollars in my bank account, but God provides, so I trusted.

It was interesting how this domino effect continued. These tugs at my heart to give just a little bit more would not stop. My now husband and I decided that instead of giving each other Christmas presents that year, we were going to "give each other" an Operation Christmas Child box. I bought presents for a girl, and he bought presents for a boy. We both knew we had everything we needed, so why not use the money we would have spent on each other for someone who *really* needed it?

Another Sunday, there was a food drive at church. Like I said, typically, I would just ignore this announcement, but conviction got the best of me again. I bought about ten one-dollar canned goods and brought them in to donate. I started to find spare cash in my wallet and would drop a five- or ten-dollar bill into the tithing bowl during the offering time at church. It wasn't every single

Sunday, but I never carry cash so when some did come my way, I would try to give it to the church. Opportunity after opportunity arose for me to give, and every time I did, this rush of anxiety overcame me. How the heck was I going to make it when God seemed to just want me to give all my money away? Every time that anxiety crept in, a rush of peace would follow. God is good when we obey, and I had to trust that someone else needed the resources more than I did.

The obeying piece can be hard. There can be a big difference in the feelings between giving to someone you know, giving to someone in need, and giving to someone you don't think likes you because *they* need it.

Let me explain. It's fun to give to people we love. Christmas time is always my favorite. I love putting special thought and consideration into gift-giving. Even though I have never been able to afford a lot, I have always thrived off choosing gifts that I know people will appreciate. Giving to someone in need feels good. It might be a little more difficult because you have no personal connection with this person, but giving to a stranger who needs your resources more than you do can bring a lot of joy. Giving to an enemy or to someone who you think could care less about you is hard—like *really* hard. Why should you do something nice for someone that might not even like you? Well, because God says to love *everyone*.

But I say unto you, love your enemies,
bless them that curse you, do good to

them that hate you, and pray for them which despitefully use you, and persecute you. (Matthew 5:44)

And on one particular day, that is exactly what I did. I won't go into too much detail, but I know this girl who I don't think ever really cared for me much. I'm not really sure why, and I don't have actual proof of this, but I always felt that way around her. One day, this girl posted somewhere that she was in need of hygiene materials to take on a trip to donate. I saw her post and did not think much of it at first. And then the blasted conviction.

I love her just as much as I love you. Regardless of how she feels about you, you are called to love and give anyway.

That night, I drove to the store and bought some materials for her. It was not easy to get myself to give up my own time and money to do something for a person that I didn't even think liked me. I messaged her, and we met up so I could give them to her. She said thank you, and we went our separate ways. It was obvious that she was surprised I did that for her. I know I was surprised that I actually followed through with it. If it was entirely my choice, my flesh would have been tempted to say no. But I did it for Him. I did it because those are the ways that we shine God's love the brightest. I did it to bring joy to the Lord which in turn brought joy to me. And how cool was it that I had the opportunity to spread God's love through helping someone that totally didn't see it coming? It's those moments where Jesus is applauding us the loudest and giving us the "well done" nod.

I don't tell these stories to brag. I don't tell these stories to make it seem like I'm wasting the little amount of money that I do have on everyone else. Some might say it was irresponsible of me to spend any money on anyone besides myself because of my lack of a substantial income at that point in my life. But I did it because I felt called to, and I know that everything I have is because of Jesus. I did it because He always provides, and He won't leave me stranded.

I listen to this podcast called *Living on the Edge with Chip Ingram* regularly. In one particular episode, Chip talks about how, when he was in bible school, he was making $1,000/month working full-time and taking classes while his wife was home with their kids. One day, he felt convicted to donate monthly to a child in need (like a Compassion International type of thing). He didn't understand it. He didn't know how he was going to afford it. But he did it. He did it because he was being faithful to what the Lord wanted Him to do even if that meant stepping way out of his financial comfort zone. He did what he was asked and trusted that God would provide.

In another one of Chip's stories, he talks about another moment in bible school where he and his wife felt convicted to give. I can't remember the story word-for-word, but I do know he was in the same situation financially as the first story. Chip and his wife felt the need to pay for a single mom's rent, so they did. Now here is the cool part.

When their rent was close to due (or maybe it was the exact due date), Chip and his wife received a check in the mail from one of Chip's former students from when he was a teacher earlier in his lifetime. This student was a professional athlete and wrote Chip a check saying that he was new to Christ and felt the urge to mail that check. Needless to say, that check was an answer to prayer for Chip and his family after they obeyed a conviction from God that they seriously couldn't afford. God always provides.

Have you felt a conviction similar to mine and to Chip's before? Did you listen to it? Or did you ignore it because you were afraid to lose something? Did you choose your comfort zone over obeying something that God called you to do? Have you ever thought about how truly blessed you are and how giving something so small might bless someone else's life?

Life is short. Giving is good. God provides, so we should too.

A Giving Heart Is a Happy Heart

As a culture, we are extremely selfish. I know that's a blunt statement, but that's honestly how I feel. Tough love, right? Perhaps this is how I feel more directly about my generation specifically. But I think generally speaking as a whole, our society is focused on how much we can get, but we fail to give just as much or more.

I'm not just talking about money either. It can be time, resources, skills, etc. Giving is often an obligation for receiving. It's not very often in places other than the church or volunteer organizations that you see people giving just out of love and the simplicity to give.

I think our world has created this obsession with the self, and we truly sometimes think that earth revolves around us. I'm perfectly guilty of this as well. Life seems to be all about how everything affects us and what we can gain. I think it's a mindset that our culture has developed over time. We have become so preoccupied with our own little worlds that we forget anyone else matters. And I truly believe this will only get worse in the generations to come.

I understand that we're busy. I recognize that sometimes, we don't feel like we have much to offer. We have so much going on that it's hard sometimes to cut out the time. Or it's stressful to think about adding a "giving percentage" out of our paycheck. I, 100 percent, understand these things from a poor college student's perspective.

However, the thing we are missing is by having these excuses, who and/or what are we *really* worshipping?

I heard on one of Chip's podcasts that we either worship God or money. And I believe it goes further than this. We worship either God or not only money but also what money can buy, the comfort and security it can bring, and how it can benefit *us* entirely.

It's not just about what God can help us with or bless us with but also about how we can be used to bless others.

I think we not only sometimes find ourselves

worshipping money but we also hold hostage the gifts that God has blessed us with that we can use to help other people. We miss the point that this life we have been given is not solely about *us* and what *we* can get out of it. It's not just about what God can help us with or bless us with but also about how we can be used to bless others.

One thing I have recently realized is that where God might lead me someday might not be for my benefit, hardly at all. He might put me somewhere so I can bless the lives of others in whatever ways He can use me. It's about what I can *give* to people, not what I can *get*. Because of this realization, I have started to try to focus on what He can do through me to benefit the lives of anyone who needs something that I have to offer rather than focusing only on my personal gain.

We always want the best benefit. We want our cake and to eat it too. But we fail to think about God's big picture. God uses people. Often. Like *really* often. Maybe because we aren't giving what God is asking of us, someone else's prayers are not getting answered. Have you ever thought about that before? I don't say that to provoke guilt but just to get us thinking about how deeply important it is to give what we have to other people when we are asked to do so. We could be holding hostage a beautiful piece to someone else's puzzle simply because of our selfish desires.

God provides for a reason. God blesses us when we do His good. When we think we are the poorest of poor, God reminds us that we still have a little something we can give to help someone else. It can be something as little as a meaningful conversation that requires your time and energy. It can be helping a neighbor out with your labor by snow blowing their driveway when you know they don't own one. It can be donating old clothes that don't fit anymore to a family in need. It can be giving money for offering at church. It can be whatever you are feeling called to give. Our world needs more of that.

Give and it will be given to you. (Luke 6:38)

How much simpler can this promise be? Give your time, your money, your resources, your "whatever" that God is calling you to surrender, and He will bless you. He will provide. He will protect. He will guide. He will not leave you or forsake you. He uses us to bless others. Let Him use you. He *will* give back to you if you obey His calling to give.

Honor the Lord with your wealth, with the
first fruits of all of your crops. (Proverbs 3:9)

I love this verse. It emphasizes the decision to worship Him and give Him your absolute best, first and foremost. To honor God, we have to trust Him. We have to have faith in His greater plan and submit to whatever He calls us to give because our whole purpose is to serve Him. Our goal in our Christian lives is to answer our callings to fulfill the greater plan that we might not understand. And we don't have to understand. God is in control, and we just have to trust that

His blueprint is much better and more meaningful than our own. And to really wholeheartedly believe and live out that faith means to listen to Him when he asks us to sacrifice.

When we don't understand why, He wants us to *do it anyway.*

When we're scared of what will happen if we do listen, *do it anyway.*

He will bless you for obeying His requests.

If we really want to be like Jesus we need to give like He does.

If we really want to be like Jesus, we need to give like He does. You will find greater joy by listening to the Lord's convictions rather than running away from them. You will find peace in knowing that what you gave meant something to someone and had an impact whether you personally got to experience the difference it had or not. Rest assured that when you give generously and focus on what you have to offer rather than what you can gain, life is much more joyful. You will find so much more fulfillment. Not only will you love yourself more, but God will also be head over heels excited and proud of you because you did something that maybe wasn't easy but meant a whole lot more in heaven than it ever will on earth.

Give because He thinks so highly of you that He has asked you to personally bless someone else with *your* gifts.

Give because it fills yours and God's heart with so much joy.

Give because He gives to you even when you don't deserve it.

Give because He always provides for all your needs.

Give because our goal is to spread God's love and what better way to do that than to show a simple act of kindness by surrendering yourself to fulfill a calling to serve others and the greater plan.

CHAPTER 7

A Busy Schedule
Defines Success

THE JAM-PACKED PLANNER

It was August of 2018. It was the beginning of a new semester. A fresh school year meant new classes, a new schedule, new responsibilities, and a brand-new internship. I was excited, nervous, and ready to learn.

During the first or second time being at my internship, the wonderfully generous company I would be working for bought a catered lunch to welcome the new interns (sidenote: I cannot say enough how sweet these people were). All the employees asked us questions about what we wanted to do, what we were interested in, what our majors were, and the golden question: What do you do in your free time?

There were three interns total, including me. The other girl intern went first. She said she loved to work out and that was all she really had time for between work and school.

The guy intern went next, and when everyone looked at him eager to hear his answer, he responded with, "What is free time?"

Everyone laughed as if in agreement that they all lacked free time as well. Then all the heads turned toward me.

"I actually do have a good chunk of free time. I love to read, workout, spend time with my dog, and relax," I said this a little bit bolder than I thought it out in my head.

You would have thought I spoke a different language by the looks on everyone's faces.

I remember thinking how odd to me it was that these were the reactions that I was getting. Did nobody else value their free time? Or did everyone else keep themselves too busy so they truly did not have any? Maybe they did have free time but were just shocked when I talked about mine in a way that emphasized how important it was to me.

What they didn't know is that it wasn't always a priority for me. I used to be the girl whose planner was booked out every hour. I was once the girl who stared at her to-do lists and cried until my eyes were puffy because I thought being busy was just how life had to be. I was once fascinated by the person who spent time going on walks with their significant others and reading books. But I felt like I had to stay busy all the time—literally, *all the time.* I craved it. A full schedule meant I was on my way to success…or so I thought.

So as you can imagine (or perhaps the procrastinators can't resonate with this, ha ha, love you all!) most semesters when organizing my planner, my to-do lists were at least a page or two long. I had plans booked months in advance, and I would write out a tentative schedule for the upcoming week every Sunday. I would have notes written out at the top of every page for every little detail of my life "so I wouldn't forget." I would tack on more responsibilities than I could *really* handle because I felt like I needed to do everything and "get ahead" of everyone else by doing more. If I noticed a day where I had free time, I would be sure to try to find something to fill that open space. I was *obsessed* with planning and being on the go at all times—very type A.

I was terrified to slow things down. It made me anxious to think about being alone with my own thoughts. I kept busy because I thought it made me happy, but it actually made me feel quite the opposite. And ironically, I was too *busy* to notice how I really felt with a loaded-up life. I was anxious all the time. I would go to bed on edge and wake up already stressed out. I was unhappy. I was trying to fill a void through working more, studying more, and adding more obligations to my life. The busier I was, the less time I had to think about my mental state, and the even less time I had to be alone with my mind to think about the things I was trying to push down deep. I was more irritable and gave off a colder vibe to my loved ones. "I didn't have time to care" was my mindset. I was focused on me and my schedule, and goodbye to anyone and everyone that stood in my way because I "had to get these things done." In a nutshell, I was a stressed, overorganized, hot *mess*.

This way of life was all that I knew from the time I was in high school until a few years into college. High school was a busy time because I was involved in extracurricular activities and sports. School, practice, homework, bed, repeat—I was that girl (and still can be) who would bawl her eyes out because I was too busy and felt like I had no time to be exceptional in one area out of all the things I was involved in. But I kept doing it because I thought this was normal and what I had to do to be successful. Then I graduated. Because I had been hyper-involved in different activities throughout high school, when I got to college, I went insane and developed an overwhelming amount of anxiety because I "needed to be busy."

Think about this. You're in high school, and you're filling out college or job applications, and you see the question, What are your hobbies? If you were a high school athlete, I guarantee you probably wrote down all the sports you participated in and had no idea what else a "hobby" was.

I think this is interesting. Granted, when you're in high school, your parents might have wanted you to participate in a lot of extra things to keep you out of trouble. Also, when you're that age, you're getting a taste of what your interests are. So I do understand why many high school students don't know exactly what else to put for that question. However, I also think that from a young age, we are taught that a busy lifestyle is the *only* lifestyle. We forget to stop and smell the flowers. We are always on missions to accomplish tasks and keep our schedules full because the key to the *American Dream* is to work as hard as we possibly can for success, right? Or perhaps we stay so busy to keep ourselves occupied so we don't have to *think* about the problems or empty holes in our lives?

If you look back at the sixth paragraph of this chapter where I talk about how obsessed with keeping busy I was, you'll notice that I said, "I used to be that girl." *Used to,* as in past tense, I still am and always will be a big-schedule type of person. I like to know what's going on and have things written down. My planner is still overwhelming for people who don't understand how my brain works. Nothing wrong with that. But is my planner as full as it used to be? That is the big question. And my answer to that, fortunately, is no.

However, I will admit that I still find myself getting caught up in wanting to be involved in as many things as I can sometimes. I'm human, and it's a habit that I have unfortunately developed. But you'll see later in this chapter how I have been able to slowly work at resetting my brain. It takes baby steps sometimes, and that's okay.

Rewind to the seventh paragraph where I talk about being OCD about planning out my semesters. Specifically, I'm talking about semesters previous to fall 2018 when my internship occurred (I know I'm making you flip back to the beginning twice, but it's all important; I promise). The summer before this semester had started, I had finally learned why I was so overwhelmed and how to slow things down in my life. I thought about what my goals were and why I was doing what I was doing. How could I cut things out to give myself more time to find peace? What was *really* important, and what was *essential* for me to take on in the next four months? I was approaching this coming schedule differently than I had in the past. It took self-control. It took talking myself through what really mattered. It took me telling myself over and over again that saying no is okay.

Absolute-no-room-to-budge essentials for the semester included my internship and some classes. I needed to get those things done, no question. I cut out pretty much all clubs and extracurriculars. I set aside time for a bible study group (changed my world), my family, my now husband, and tried to spend as much time as I could learning how to develop my relationship with Jesus. More time for peace. Less stress. Best decisions ever. I make it seem like it was super easy to do, but it was *very* challenging and hard to make that mindset switch. And like I said, I find myself falling into old habits sometimes, and that is when I have to take a step back and reevaluate why I'm doing what I'm doing and what *really* deserves my attention.

What were my real honest reasons for trying to keep busy? And what happened when I did sit still? Why did my crazy schedule make me so unhappy, and why did the thought of utter silence give me anxiety?

To keep it simple, my heart and my busy tasks did not align with God's plan. I was go-go-going to keep myself from having time to listen to Jesus's voice. I was doing my life my way, and I was miserable doing it. Peace and quiet meant that the Holy Spirit had time to convict me, and I wanted no part of that. I wanted "success," and I wanted nothing to do with God's agenda for my life, so I made my own and made it packed with things that "successful" college kids do.

Are you keeping busy to avoid a conviction?

Evaluate your life. Look at your schedule. Think about your "whys" and how they make you feel. Are you doing things for you or for the greater plan? Are you keeping busy to avoid a conviction? Are you chasing after the American Dream by doing all these things to seek worldly success? Is your busy life bringing you peace? Or do you need to slow down, say no, and give yourself time with Jesus to find the life balance that you crave? The fulfillment that you need? The purpose that you're searching for?

THE JOY OF PEACE

Have you ever been completely alone in your home with absolutely nothing to do? I know that's a general question, and most of you are probably thinking there is *always* something to do at home. But what I mean is have you ever sat in your home and just taken the time to sit in quiet and just listen? Ignoring the to-do list, no phones, no TV, kids napping, dog's outside, just you. If you're like I was, it makes you anxious or uncomfortable. You can't sit still, and you have an itch to get up and do something or find a distraction. Whether that something is productive or a waste of time, you just can't seem to let your brain rest in peace.

Why is that?

You might feel similar to how I did. I was overwhelmed and miserable. Feeling overwhelmed can be normal at times, but the problem was my *why*. I was living life task after task with no fulfillment. I was doing life the way that *I* wanted. And that way of living is exhausting, purposeless, and extremely stressful. I was avoiding quiet because conviction would set in, and I did not want to listen. I didn't want to hear God tell me that I needed to slow down. I was being selfish and creating my own misery by planning my life around events that I thought were bringing value to my life. I was being rebellious against a plan that is *so* much greater than I can imagine because I wanted control. I was missing out on beautiful peace for a sad busy schedule that the enemy whispered in my ear was the key to success.

Our culture tells us that the more things we have going on, the more "normal" we are. The more we load our schedules up, the happier we will be. The busier we are, the more successful we will be.

But I'm here to tell you that life is not meant to be lived that way. Busyness happens. But when it becomes a lifestyle that is centered around the self and what *we* can constantly gain, that is the issue that will leave you feeling empty. Life can be a lot to manage sometimes, but joy is still present if life is being lived for Jesus, His perfect plan for our lives, and for the greater good of His glory.

By the seventh day, God had completed
His work, so He rested. (Genesis 2:2)

God *rested*. He didn't keep going until he was beyond the point of burnout. He rested and gave Himself time to rejuvenate. We need time to fill our cups. We can't pour love and purpose running on empty. Your laundry can wait. Your kids can pick one sport. You time, family time, Jesus time, and complete utter rest time are all essential to a life of contentment. It's not easy, and I would say most people think this is a crazy way to live. But if you only knew. If you only knew the joy and fulfillment it would bring, you would understand how important it is to *rest*.

Come to me, all who labor and are heavy laden, and I will give you rest. (Matthew 11:28)

Having trouble allowing yourself to rest? Seek God and ask for Him to show you how. I struggle with this a lot. When I find myself overdoing it and can't seem to find it in myself to sort out my own priorities, I ask God to *show* me how to relax and slow down. I boldly pray about it and ask Him to make it obvious what I don't need to be involved in.

Be still and know that I am God. (Psalm 46:10)

We are called to be still and allow God to do His works in our lives. We aren't called to live busy schedules so we can avoid a calling because it doesn't work with our controlling mindsets. To find peace, we have to slow down and let Jesus do His thing. We have to obey convictions and seek His callings. We have to wait and trust in the times of the unknown. THIS is how we feel joy in *all* circumstances. THIS is how we find the peace we're all searching for. THIS is how we find our purpose and fulfillment. Rest. Listen. Do.

Knowing what I know now about the beautiful peace I can experience, I will never again deprive myself for too long of time to slow down, and more importantly, Jesus time. I recognize when I'm becoming too busy and not setting aside time to spend with God. I feel the joy fade; the stress increases, and my life becomes more frustrating. You need to fill your cup before you can ever wholeheartedly fill someone else's. Don't shut out the opportunity for God to speak to your heart by loading up your life. American culture says busyness is the key to success, but Jesus calls us to rest; be still, and seek Him for *real* success.

American culture says busyness is the key to success but Jesus calls us to rest, be still, and seek Him for real success.

CHAPTER 8

Vulnerability Is Weakness

THE STRUGGLE

I had two internships during my senior year of college: fall semester and winter semester. The first one you already know about from the chapter before this with a wellness company (if you didn't know it was a wellness company then you do now). My second one was with a fitness company, and it was hands down—one of the most eye opening, challenging, fun, and incredible experiences I have ever had. I'll explain.

This company was and is the kind of business who truly cares about their employees. They literally are like a giant family, and everyone loves everyone. They laugh a ton. The positive energy is through the roof. The way they care about their clients is so personal. They *actually* believe and live out their core values. Respect and love are just expected. I cannot say enough kind words about the priorities of the company and the people who work there.

As a brand-new intern, I was excited to be a part of this awesome place, but I did expect to be treated a little lower on the totem pole. I think that's what we all kind of expect as interns, right? But this company did quite the opposite. They went over the top making me and all of my fellow eleven interns feel appreciated and included. We were taught leadership development and personal training presentations every week. The intentionality of our leaders to learn our names and personal things about us was something like I had never experienced before in a work environment. Not to mention that we were *interns,* so who knows if they were ever going to see us again after the semester was over. They cared, and it showed.

Throughout my time at this extraordinary place, the growth that took place in my life was desperately needed. My attitude was affected. My outlook on life was altered. My perception on the importance of body language had changed. It was all for the better. I was a smiley happy girl and felt like I was working toward the person I wanted to be and felt in my heart I was supposed to be. The positive impact was amazing. I met some incredible Christ-loving individuals that I will always hold near and dear to my heart. It blows my mind how God places us in situations that we never thought we would be in and surrounds us with people that we needed for that time frame in our lives when we least expect it. It was blatantly obvious that God placed me in that specific internship for reasons I never would have been able to piece apart on my own—one reason being the theme of this chapter that I will be getting to soon.

Out of all the life-changing events that I participated in with this company, there was one specific day and one particular presentation that *really* hit me. We talked about vulnerability in the workplace and with clients. Specifically, we talked about the power of sharing our weaknesses and how that can create strong connections between people.

The instructor paired each of us interns with another. I'm assuming he probably put us together based on our interaction thus far in the semester, meaning if you hadn't talked too much to each other, you were probably partners.

Here is how the exercise went. We sat directly across from our partners to make it super personal and intimate. One partner was told to tell a super happy story that had occurred in their life within the last year while the other partner who would be the listener was told to completely ignore the person telling the story. The point was to make us understand the frustrating and lonely feeling of not being cared about when you want to share something to someone that is meaningful to you. We switched roles, discussed how it made us feel, and that was the end of round one.

Round two is what hit home. The partner who would first be the storyteller (opposite of the partner who was first to tell the happy story in round one) was told to tell about a deep, personal, and upsetting event that had occurred at some point in their life. Details and emotions were the key here. The listener was told to be as empathetic and comforting as possible to make their partner feel as cared about as they could. The idea this time was to understand how it feels to give someone your undivided attention when people are talking to you about things that might not be easy to talk about and mean a whole lot to them. The goal was to feel the connection that can develop from discussing weaknesses and to recognize the importance of empathy in developing trust and relationships.

My stomach dropped a little bit when we were first told what we were supposed to do. I'm sure everyone was nervous to get real and deep with a stranger, but it was kind of odd personally for me to feel that way. I'm usually an open book about my life (as you can probably tell by now), but to be that personal with someone I hardly knew face-to-face was a little intimidating. I have a big heart for people, so the caring about my partner piece was going to be right up my alley, but to share my story was the challenge.

Needless to say, I did it anyway, and my partner was super sweet about making me feel like my personal trauma mattered. Regardless if it meant anything to him, he made me feel like my feelings were valid, and I appreciated that. In a nutshell, he nailed the exercise.

There was one little problem with the story I chose to tell. It *was* deep, and it *was* sad, but it wasn't one of those things that is *super* hard for me to talk about with a stranger. I talked about my parents' divorce and how it had impacted me and different situations that had occurred over the course of their separation. Yes, it was an upsetting topic. Yes, it left a huge impact on my life. Yes, it was a traumatizing event. However, it wasn't like pulling teeth and emotion provoking for me to share that experience. And just a quick sidenote, I think this is because it wasn't recent, and the wounds from that event had pretty much scarred over at that point in my life.

What was the problem with this? I didn't give my partner the same opportunity for connection that he gave me. I did not give him my full trust, and I chose not to talk about something that was buried deep and difficult for me to share. Instead, I remained more surface level.

He told me an extremely personal occurrence in his life that he had hardly shared with anyone. He struggled to find the words. I could see the questioning of my trust in his eyes when he first started telling his story. Tears rolled down his face as he was telling me about his traumatic event. I asked questions. I hugged him. I did my best to make him feel loved and comfortable. It was natural for me to give him all of my attention because personal connection is something I value, and comfort is something I love to give. But I had robbed him of the opportunity to feel what I had felt on a connection level. The vulnerability he had shared with me had allowed me to care about him in a way that I wasn't sure was possible because of my lack of knowing him. But I did not give him that opportunity in return. While I cannot directly speak for this person, my guess is that he could probably tell I was being more superficial than he was with my story and that cost the relationship.

So what is my point with this story and all of this vulnerability stuff? How does this all connect? Through that story with my partner, I realized the real potential and value that vulnerability holds. I think the world makes us think that bringing down the walls around our hearts is being imperfect and fragile. Vulnerability itself is *not* weakness. It opens up the opportunity to create relationships and relate to people in ways we might have never thought was possible. We have no idea what we might have in common with another person and what being open and honest about our struggles could create with that individual.

I clammed up. I held back. I told myself that I could not get deep with a stranger for fear of rejection and judgement. I was afraid to appear "weak." I didn't want someone I didn't know to look at me and know that I struggle too. I cared more about my appearance and pride than the connection and potential difference I could make with this person by allowing him into my heart.

God values intimate relationships. He calls us to community. He commands us to love the way that Jesus loved. He wants us to be united through Him. We are all brothers and sisters in Christ and need to treat each other as such. But how can we do that when we're too afraid to connect with people for fear of appearing "weak"? How can we *really* develop trust with each other when we're too focused on what everyone will

> We are united through our differences, our struggles, our challenges, and our hurt.

think if we share our imperfect parts? How can we *truly* connect if we keep building the walls up rather than tearing them down? We are united through our differences, our struggles, our challenges, and our hurt. But why are we all trying so hard to paint a pretty picture for everyone else to cover up our flaws? Honest, open, vulnerable hearts are the key to connections, relationships, and the will of the Lord.

Ask yourself this. Are you pushing your "stuff" down deep? Are you hiding from your weaknesses? Or are you embracing them? Recognize the beauty of vulnerability and not only the freedom it can bring for you but also the relationships that can develop and grow when you pour out your heart at the right place and time.

THE BEAUTY

Struggling sucks. I mean it *really* sucks. Every single person can attest to that. Being challenged and stretched can be uncomfortable. Coping with unfortunate situations can be painful. Being tested can be frustrating. We all know that dealing with our "stuff" is hard. It's confusing. It's sometimes depressing. We wonder why these things happen to us and question what the "good" is in our poor circumstances. Why does God allow bad things to happen to good people? Why can't He perform miracles for every sickness, broken marriage, and financial struggle? Why can't following Jesus be all sunshine and rainbows *all* the time?

The answer to these questions has taken *a lot* of time and *a lot* of faith for me to understand. I used to think that the definition of being a Christian meant a peaceful, happy, struggle-free life 95 percent of the time. The other 5 percent was for God's wrath when He was "mad" at me. I thought life would be easier, and God would bless me with less difficulties because I chose to follow Him. Unless of course if I committed a "big sin" then came all the real wrath. What a distorted vision, huh?

Some people might agree that they thought or do think similarly to how I did. Life gets hard, and all of a sudden, God is a monster or not real because He's supposed to protect us from hardship, right? We expect that He's always going to dish us out of the "crap." And when He doesn't, we question everything. We get mad at God. We resent Him. We think, *Why us?* when we've done nothing to deserve this "punishment" that God has shunned us with.

I'm not saying that it's not normal to feel angry when random bad things happen. I get that. I've been there too. What I'm questioning is the perspective and *who* we should really be angry with.

Our God is an incredibly *loving* Father. The amount of love He has for us is immeasurable. He has the kind of heart that we will never fully understand and loves in a way that we will never be able to wrap our heads around. He loves you, and He loves me *so* much that He sent His *only* son to die for us.

Think about that for a second. God has one son—one single son. And He sent Jesus to be beaten, tortured, and hung on a cross for our sins for each and every person to have the opportunity to meet Him in heaven someday. He sent Jesus to die for sins that would be committed years and years later. He watched the thorns pierce Jesus's head, the whips break the skin on his back, and the nails get hammered into his wrists and feet. If you're a parent or if you're not, put yourself in the mindset that you are and ask yourself if you would give your child that burden to help people you don't even know. *That* is how much God loves us.

My point is God isn't out to punish us or by any means enjoys seeing us struggle. When we cry, He cries. When we're frustrated, He hears our frustrations. When we feel like we have nothing left to give and all hope is lost, He is right there with us. If this is true, then why does He allow awful things to happen? Why do we sometimes feel like we're walking this life surrounded by darkness with no light at the end of the tunnel?

Trust. Desperation. Growth. Those are the methods behind the perceived madness.

Trust and desperation go hand in hand. Trials occur, and these are the times when God wants us to cry out for Him. He wants to know and for us to admit that we still need Him. He wants us to trust the process and remember that He has our lives in His hands. *Always.* If we never experience hurting hearts and longing for answers, then some of us might forget who is really in control. Some of us tend to shove God under the rug more often when life is wonderful and going our way. Sometimes we need a wake-up call. Sometimes we need to endure pain and what feels like unanswered prayers to get down on our knees and give Him back the remote to our lives.

I'm not saying God punishes us for enjoying life. I'm saying that sometimes we get comfortable doing life *our* way and not seeking the Lord or asking for directions for His will. We start to live life solely for our benefit, and we slowly slip away from spending time with Jesus. Sometimes our lives come crashing down, so we can humbly cry out for help and remember to trust in His plan.

Besides testing our trust, sometimes God allows us to be in unfortunate situations to stretch our character. Life molds us—the good stuff and the bad stuff. And sometimes, we need to endure the bad stuff to transform into the person that God wants us to be. We all have a special purpose. And what if to fulfill that purpose our hearts and minds need to be altered?

For example, what if you're meant to lead a special group that helps others cope with the loss of a parent? You obviously would not be able to relate to people who have suffered that kind of loss if you yourself have not had to go through it. This is God's way of using something tragic to create something beautiful. And what if leading that group gave you a sense of fulfillment that you had never experienced before? You would have found a godly purpose. A godly purpose that you would not have been able to serve if you had not equally suffered the loss of a parent.

My point is that God allows horrible things to occur for reasons we might not understand at the time but are always for the good in the long run. Running away from God is never the answer. Hold on to Jesus tighter than ever and trust that there is a beautiful purpose for your struggle.

> Blessed is the man who remains steadfast under trial, for when he has stood the test he will receive the crown of life, which God has promised to those who love him. (James 1:12)

So what does this have to do with vulnerability? Well, everything.

We feel the most connected when we relate to each other's challenges. We can use tragedies or low points in our lives to help others remember that there is a reason for what they are going through even if they can't see it right now. Remember the example I used about losing a parent? Well, in order for that tragic event to help anyone become a beautiful blessing and fulfill a godly purpose, a vulnerable heart has to be present. We have to talk about our hardships *out loud*. We have to support and love one another as we open up our hearts and talk about the hurt that most of us don't want to talk about. It's okay to be soft. It's okay to be loving. It's okay to be vulnerable. It is not weakness.

> I appeal to you, brothers and sisters, in the name of our Lord Jesus Christ, that all of

you agree with one another in what you say and that there be no divisions among you, but that you be perfectly united in mind and thought. (1 Corinthians 1:10)

Carry each other's burdens, and in this way you will fulfill the law of Christ. (Galatians 6:2)

God created you carefully and perfectly with all of your "stuff."

We are called to community, to build relationships, and to carry the burdens of others. In other words, we are called to support and encourage each other through the hurt. We cannot fulfill this request from Jesus by following the world's view of vulnerability as a weakness. We don't have to have it all together, and we sure as heck don't have to act like we do. We don't have to go through things alone. We need each other. And we need to change this distorted view that opening up our hearts to talk about our problems means we're lesser than others or "imperfect." God created you carefully and perfectly with all of your "stuff." You have no idea how sharing your struggles could change someone else's world or, better yet, bring them to know our Jesus.

And we *must* stop judging one another for those imperfections. Jesus loves you just as much as he loves the person you are judging. Nobody is better than anyone else. We are *all* sons and daughters, brothers and sisters in Christ.

Be the real you, junk and all. Let God be the judge. He knows your heart. He knows your deepest struggles. And He also knows how you can use those struggles for good. Don't let the enemy win by holding everything in or shaming yourself for your challenges. Seek God's Word and remember that He always turns the worst circumstances into a way of fulfillment. He has the power to rebuild our hearts. Let Him.

And ask God to work on helping you chip off the hardened pieces surrounding your heart that are preventing you from reaching out to others. Ask Him to give you the opportunities to build relationships and get connected. Pray that He opens doors for you to share your "stuff" with others to help rebuild them as well. Learn to live with a vulnerable heart that seeks Jesus, and you will surely change lives. You will build connections and relationships that you might not know the purpose for at the time, but there are reasons that are much higher than our own understanding. You will lead people to the Prince of Peace and to a world they might not have ever known had you not taken a leap of faith and opened up your heart.

CHAPTER 9

Everybody has Sex

FALSE PERFECTION

Boy, oh boy! This is the chapter I have been dreading since the day that I decided to write this book. This is the chapter of pure and brutal honesty. This is the ultimate test of vulnerability for me because this has been one of the deepest and truest struggles of my life. I *will* be blunt, and I *will* be honest. So buckle up and ready your heart to talk about a sensitive topic in my life.

Let me start by saying that God's timing is absolutely amazing to me. I took a little break while writing this book because I had a lot of big milestones occur that took up a lot of my time (college graduation, wedding, moving, starting graduate school, etc.). Not a day went by that I didn't think about how badly I knew I needed to finish writing. However, for this topic specifically, I wasn't ready to talk about it six months ago. I was terrified and feeling unworthy to talk about God's grace over a subject that I had always struggled to understand. This break was exactly what I needed to find the words to write this chapter and finish this book. I needed to experience what I have in order to speak this truth to the best of my ability.

When I decided to follow the calling to write this book, the first thing that I did was brainstorm which topics I wanted to talk about. I wanted to dig deep about my struggles that revolved around societal views and be completely open about things I knew other people had to have dealt with or are currently dealing with. I knew I wasn't the only one, but I also knew that God was calling me to talk about the grace and freedom that He provides. I needed to talk about the secrets and struggles of my heart, but I also needed to talk about God's redemption and love. I knew in my heart that God was calling me to speak His truth about worldly "norms" and what God *really* says about these topics. This was one subject I automatically had a pull on my heart to talk about. I didn't want to. I didn't know how to. But I knew I had to. American culture tells us that we shouldn't talk about it out loud, but I felt a push to talk about it anyway and share what I have learned. This topic, sex, has taken me a lot of time to understand, and I'm excited (and nervous) to share my truth with you.

Step one of this truth-telling process has to begin with me being extremely honest about my sexual life. So my "number" is two. For those who don't understand what I mean by number, this is terminology that my generation uses to put a numerical value on how many guys or girls they have had sex with. And again, mine is two.

That's hard for me to admit. Here I am writing a book about God's truth, and I'm telling you not only did I not wait for marriage but also I have had sex with two different people. If you are in my boat or if your number is much higher than mine or if you just lost your virginity to a boyfriend or girlfriend, please hear me out. Your number does not define you. Your number does not make you unworthy. Your number is not something you're meant to carry around with you like a ball and chain.

I carried mine like a ball and chain for a long time. I lost my virginity to a boyfriend when I was in high school. I wasn't ready, but in my "well, society says it's okay" mindset, I convinced myself that I was.

The enemy does a really nice job of covering up God's truth with a false image of perfection and security. I thought giving up my virginity would make everything about my high school relationship perfect. I thought that we would be together forever; therefore, it was okay that I let it happen. Friends around me talked about how awesome it was, so I figured something so great must be okay to do.

But no one talked about the emptiness, unworthiness, and frustration that comes with it. Does everyone experience these negative emotions? I'm not sure. Some people might be a lot better at stuffing them away and pretending that they don't exist, but someone like me who has a hard time shutting my emotions off, I let those feelings I experienced run my world. I thought because I was no longer a virgin that meant I was no longer able to associate myself as being a Christian. I thought I was unworthy of God's love and that His grace couldn't wash away that sin. And I *really* thought that I would never be able to find a good man who wanted a girl that gave away something so special.

This sin affected my whole way of pursuing my relationship with God. There was me. Then there was God. And right in between us was this wedge of sexual sin. The shame caused me to distance myself, and I allowed the emptiness to consume my life. It prevented me from being able to grow in Christ. At some points, I would feel a nudge in my heart and would slowly make my way back to talking with God; however, I could only get so close until the conviction would settle in. I would get angry. Why couldn't I have sex and have a good relationship with God? He created it, didn't he? I couldn't understand why it was "bad" in the first place. The "rules" of sex were something I could never wrap my head around. Why is something so good "forbidden" in God's eyes until marriage? Why is this thing that brings emotional closeness frowned upon until you say I do? And if God appears to be against sex before marriage, then why has our society normalized it?

I'm sure these are questions you may have struggled with as well. Like I said earlier, it has taken me time to get a better grasp at the answers to these questions. So here I am today ready to dive right in.

How It Was Intended

God is a sex cheerleader at its right time.

I have done a lot of digging and learning about how God views sex. My biggest takeaway from all that I have pieced together is this: God is a sex cheerleader *at its right time.* I used to picture God as this anti-sex hater for lack of a better term that shunned one and all who participated. I used to think He just hated sex and wanted everyone who experienced it to feel guilty about it because I thought of it as a "dirty" act. But I'm a little bit older now and have learned so much about what God *actually* says about sex. God created sex, and He is FOR sex under the covenant of marriage. He knows how important it is and knows the emotional passion that results from it. He wants that for me and for you.

He created it to be this beautiful special moment between one man and one woman who chose to commit themselves to each other for the rest of their lives. It was meant to be this powerful connection to be experienced with one other person under the unity of marriage. It's one piece of the fulfillment puzzle that has to be met under certain circumstances to get the biggest bang for your buck. In other words, without God's blessing of marriage, sex is empty. You might feel the passion during the act, but afterward, you're left with nothing but circumstantial guilt and a hole in your heart that seeks something greater.

God *is* that something greater. And God created marriage to be the context where sex takes place. A dating relationship is not the same. Let me say that again, sex while you're dating is not the same. Marriage is a full-blown commitment under God to love each other no matter what circumstances arise. It is the decision to work toward oneness together as a couple. You can walk away from a dating relationship any time you please. Marriage is staying through thick and thin. Marriage is loyalty. Marriage is a special kind of love. Marriage is a different kind of passion and a different kind of sex.

The problem is that our society has taken this beautiful gift that was intended for a husband and wife and has made it a loveless act that people do to numb their current lives. It has become about how many people we can have sex with or what kind of false short-term fulfillment we can attain rather than committing to that one special person that God has chosen just for you to love and cherish for a lifetime.

So if God created sex to bring emotional fulfillment between a man and a woman, what do you do before marriage to satisfy that emotional need? This is the question that I could never wrap my head around, and my answer speaks from my understanding and experience. *Learn how to find emotional connection in other ways.*

You might not always have the opportunity to have sex to fulfill that need with your husband or wife someday. For example, what if one of you gets in an accident and is paralyzed from the waist down? That changes the game. You have to find other ways to keep that part of your marriage alive. Learn how to become intimate with one another without being physical. Find each other's love languages and act on them. Talk about the desires of your hearts. Pray for the strength to resist the temptation that so many of us fall into and for God to reveal other ways to fulfill that emotional desire.

And, sister, unless your man is extremely respectful of you and your decisions and/or is rooted in Christ, he will have a hard time understanding this. Pray for his heart and mind to be open to understanding your needs to refrain from sexual sin.

And let me take this one step further and say unless you see a future with the man you are with, don't waste yours or God's time on him. God has a special person for you, but as humans on earth, we are given the ability to make our own choices. If the man you are currently with is not someone you see yourself with and not someone that wants to see the both of you united under God, ditch him, girl, because God has someone better for you.

Let me be open and honest again when I say that my now husband and I had sex before we were married. I knew we shouldn't have, but it happened, and once it happens, it's really hard to stop. As my relationship with Jesus grew, a tug on my heart to stop became stronger. I had reached a point where I knew this sin was holding me back from spiritual growth. So I chose God and prayed for strength. Restraining from sexual acts was easily one of the hardest things that I have ever done, and we weren't perfect, but I knew in my heart that I had to give my best effort and lean on God during times of temptation.

My husband and I got married in August of 2019, and let me tell you how freeing and absolutely beautiful it is to share that moment with the love of your life, guilt-free, the way it was intended. It's an amazing experience that I encourage you to wait for.

The higher you let your number get, the harder it is to treasure and cherish the intimate gift that God created for you and one other person. The more baggage you bring to the moment, the more difficult it is to see just how perfect it is supposed to be.

So if you're someone whose number is not where you ever thought it would be or you're ashamed of it but you know in your heart that that's not how God intended sex to be, I hope you find peace in knowing that you are *so* not alone. Whether you have been with one person or twenty people, God loves you the same. Guilt and shame are not from God. They are emotions from the enemy to make you feel like you're not good enough to seek grace.

But you, my friend, are more than enough just as you are to come to the altar and allow God to free those chains. You aren't perfect, and it's extremely hard to live in a world where sex has become increasingly normal in all kinds of contexts. Our society has

But you my friend, are more than enough just as you are to come to the altar and allow God to free those chains.

downplayed its true beauty, and that is not your fault. Pour your heart into our perfect and graceful God, and He will redeem what is broken. Resistance is hard, but joy is worth it. He has someone perfectly picked out for you to endure that precious moment with that will make the wait worth your while.

I hope whoever reads this and relates to it resonates with it and finds peace and grace in a world where we often avoid talking about sex. You are defined by so much more.

I hope my imperfect past and vulnerability encourages you to seek God first and wait. I know I would have experienced sex from a much purer perspective if I would have. And if you're in the same boat that I was in, resist. God's blessing is worth it.

> Delight yourself in the Lord and He will give you the desires of your heart. (Psalm 37:4)

Put your trust in your Father and seek Him always, and He will show you at the right time how beautiful and special He intended sex to be.

CHAPTER 10

God's Plan Doesn't Exist

THE ENEMY'S INTERVENTION

Writing this book has been the scariest, hardest, and weird-est experience of my life. Scary because many days, I don't feel worthy to preach the words I'm typing. Hard because finding the time to do it is a task in itself. And weird because never did I ever see myself in this position sharing my weak points and giving God all the glory for His grace.

I never thought of writing as something I could or would ever do to this extent. I knew that my mom and dad told me when I was in fourth grade that I was good at it, and that was about it. If you would have told me five years ago that I was going to write a book, I, 100 percent, would have told you that you were a nutcase.

But sometimes God intervenes because He knows best and He has a plan that is so much bigger than us. Let me tell you the story of why and how I got to this point.

Here's a little background summary from earlier chapters: I grew up in a Christian home with parents who took my siblings and I to church regularly. My parents divorced when I was under ten years old, and my mom continued to take us to church on her weekends. My mom always has been the rock to my foundation in my faith. She's the one who has showed me from the very beginning what it looks like to love like Jesus does. This, in a super small nutshell, is where my faith was born.

Fast way forward to my senior year of college where I had finally started to understand what it meant to make my faith my own. Prior to senior year, I always knew where my heart was and how much it craved Jesus, but I was a fool for "worldly fulfillment" and found myself confused and lost more often than not. But something clicked that fall of college senior year, and I was finally on a path that started to align with the desires of my heart—the desires that God placed there. The sense of peace, overwhelming praise, and joyfulness that Jesus followers talked about, yeah, I felt that. And it felt better than I ever thought it could.

You're probably wondering what it was that clicked for me and how it happened. That's an interesting question because I've often thought about that myself and tried to pinpoint what was different about my life then that was not in previous years that pulled me toward the light.

Here's what I can tell you. First, find a community. I cannot stress this enough. I started a bible study with a group of girls who all had their struggles. We came together with the purpose of growing in Jesus as women of faith and holy cow did that change my heart What started as something that seemed like a fun thing to do turned into something I craved every week and completely changed the way my week went. I've been on the flip side of this situation where I've felt very isolated and distant. The pastor ain't lying when he says that is when the enemy attacks you full force. Find your girls. Find your guys. And stay united in Christ.

Second, spend time growing in Him. That bible study kick-started a whole new growth mindset that I had never experienced before despite being a Christian my whole life. I was on a podcast grind, a loving everyone grind, an understand the Bible grind, a reading spiritual growth books grind, and a Christian music all day everyday grind. I thrived off seeking ways to learn more about being a woman of Christ in any way that I could. It helped keep my focus on where it should be, kept me hungry to learn more, filled my cup daily, and pushed me to grow closer to Jesus. In summary, be intentional and be purposeful in your journey to grow your faith.

> Ask, and it will be given to you, seek and
> you will find, knock and it will be opened
> to you. (Matthew 7:7)

Third, listen and obey. When you are actively seeking Jesus, He wants to use you. He wants to show the whole world your heart and how that reflects who He is and how much He wants every single person to seek Him the way that you are. He wants to show them their purpose and how much they are unconditionally loved. We are called to discipleship and to talk about this amazing God that has so much more for us than we can imagine. Listen to the ways that He can use you for His glory. And when I say "listen" I'm not only talking about hearing His voice. Open your heart, your eyes, and your ears and pray about what He might be calling you to do. And the hardest but most rewarding part is to then *obey it*, no questions asked.

And that, my friend, is where you find purpose. That precious moment when God calls you and me, broken-hearted sinners, to fulfill a special mission because we have the perfect talents to do it flawlessly in his eyes (because he gave them to us) is a step in the direction of *God's plan for* your *life*. It's real. It's beautiful. It's the best decision and decisions to follow that you will ever make.

But it is just that: a decision. And decisions come with resistance from the one who wants to keep us far, far away from the peace and love of our Father. The scary thing about resistance is that it can start with one small decision to do what is more convenient for us, not what fulfills God's plan, that can lead to another similar decision that leads to another, and before we know it, we're living for us with an empty heart wondering where we went wrong.

This whole chapter so far is the definition of my writing journey. The tug on my heart to do this amazing thing that I had no confidence to do has been an extraordinarily fulfilling and beautiful experience. I was terrified to take this leap of faith, but here I am, ten chapters later, with a heart full of gratitude that God knocked on my door to do the unthinkable (in my world). He chose regular ole me to speak His truth with a whole lot of prayer and humility throughout the entire process. And the best part of me telling you this is to encourage you because *He has a job specifically for you too.*

The key is to not let resistance pull you away from what you were created to do. This was something I was not prepared for, and I never knew could take so many forms. I started writing this book with a heart full of motivation and a clear vision. The reality is life "got busy," a.k.a. other things became a priority; my confidence in God's plan decreased dramatically, and I doubted every piece and part of my ability to finish it. Resistance. Thoughts. Excuses. External and Internal. Satan is the king of holding us hostage against a fulfilling purpose and the thief of joy that tricks us into believing we are unworthy. Resistance is the enemy's way to keep us from satisfying a much greater plan that shows the world God's perfect love.

God's Plan Is Greater

The question is, where do you fit into this God's-plan puzzle, and how do you make the right decisions?

Maybe you're a new believer, and you're intrigued by this whole purpose thing. You want to feel this joy that people speak of. Here is what I recommend based on my experience:

1. Seek Jesus.
2. Pray for direction.
3. Beware of resistance.

Maybe you totally understand this battle with resistance, and you're struggling. You know what brings peace to your heart and what glorifies God, but excuses flood your schedule, and you can't seem to find the time to do what you know your heart is calling you to do.

1. Seek Jesus.
2. Pray for direction.
3. *Flee* from resistance.

In order to truly understand the path that God wants to take us on, we have to seek Him first. What does that look like? The first way I'm going to share is by going to church. Search for a place of worship that makes you feel at home. Find a holy place full of community opportunities where you can fully let God in. And keep attending. Make church a priority. If you're in a transitional phase of life or have not had the best of luck with churches, I urge you to keep looking because being united with brothers and sisters in Christ is so vital to our spiritual growth. We never know what kind of relationships God will bring into our lives, so whether you're busy, moving, or just keep finding excuses not to go, GO.

And please don't misinterpret *my* definition of church. When I hear the word *church*, my mind goes to a building where I can worship, hear sermons, and get involved. But maybe this isn't your definition. Maybe your church is a room in your house where you can have gatherings and talk about the work Jesus is doing in your lives. Or maybe your church is sitting around a bonfire on the weekends singing worship songs together. Wherever you can congregate, worship, pray, and proclaim the name of Jesus together as His people, keep doing *that*.

Seeking Jesus also means reading His Word. This is the most important piece. Reading your Bible helps you understand who God is, how much He loves you, and what He wants to do in your life. It is a gateway for communication. Find time to dig in and study. And by *study*, I mean whatever that looks like for you. When I read my Bible, I have a highlighter, journal, and a pen. First, I pray for guidance and to read whatever God feels I need in my life at that point in time. I read the words, highlight what jumps out at me, and translate it into how it applies to my life. Your bible studying might look quite a bit different from mine or feel free to use my format. Whatever works for you to feel what God wants to speak to you is the best way to read/study the Word.

And lastly, seeking Jesus means *living* like Jesus. Seeking means knowing His ways are higher than our own and surrendering our will to live the way that He intended us to live. Nobody is perfect because Jesus was the only one who lived perfectly. But I often ask myself in conflicting situations, What would Jesus do? That might sound cliché, but I'm telling you it helps. I actively think about how I think He would handle the situation I'm in, and it helps me to do things in the most loving way that I humanly know how to. I don't always succeed at portraying God's love, but I pray for strength often, and I do the best that my sinful flesh can. God doesn't expect perfection; He expects a seeking heart who desires to follow His ways and makes a conscious effort to live life the way that Jesus did with love, kindness, humility, and grace.

Once you understand the *seeking* piece, *praying for direction* makes perfect sense. If you're attending church, pray that God brings you a community and uses people to help you unravel your purpose. If you're reading your Bible, pray for the words to lead you toward what God wants to do in your life. And if you're doing your best to live like Jesus, He sees you. Pray for opportunities to show God's love and for God to reveal your gifts and how you can use them to bring Him glory. The cool thing is that if you're praying for chances to express how much God loves people, your love language to do so could directly be a God-given gift or could lead you down the path to discovering your gifts.

You're seeking, and you're praying. Maybe God is starting to carve out a path, and you're excited and feeling on fire for God. But then, the resistance hits.

Let me preface this with a little story from Matthew that I briefly mentioned earlier in this book. Just a refresh, this is the part of the Bible where Jesus was just baptized by John the Baptist, fasted for forty days and forty nights, and is tempted by the devil asking Jesus to bow down to him. The result of Satan's attempt did not work in his favor. Matthew 4:10 says, "Then Jesus said to Him, 'Away with you Satan!' For it is written 'You shall worship the Lord your God, and Him only you shall serve.'"

I don't know about you, but the kind of commitment, admiration, and love that it took for Jesus to resist Satan is incredible to me. Think about it. Jesus was just baptized, so He was vulnerable even though He already knew God. He had not eaten anything for forty days. That takes "hangry" to a whole different level. Then Jesus had Satan in His face asking Jesus to bow down to him. Yet despite all these extremely difficult circumstances, Jesus remained committed and resisted the devil because he admired and loved God so much, and He knew God deserved then and deserves now all the worship.

What would our world look like if we resisted Satan in our day-to-day lives the way that Jesus did?

We know where the opposition to obey God comes from, and it clearly is not from God. The solution? Draw closer to God and seek His Word harder than ever. Pray for the next steps to be able to fulfill the calling on your heart. Recognize what that resistance feels like, and when you notice it, try to creep back into your life, *flee*. When you hear the world tell you you're not worthy, your idea is garbage, you can never do that, etc., walk away knowing that your God is bigger than those lies that the devil places in your head and loves you too much to bring you to this life purposeless. Know that your worth in God and who He created you to be is *all* that matters.

Know that your worth in God and who He created you to be is all that matters.

God's plan is so much better than what you think is

best for your life. Every little thing about you is a result of Him crafting you in the womb and creating the perfectly imperfect person you were put on this earth to be. And you have a purpose. You have a calling to do something that only you can do.

You have a calling to do something that only you can do.

No matter how big or how small, it matters. It matters. If I could scream this in your face, I would because you need to know how much your time, money, effort, and spiritual gifts matter. I urge you to listen and pray for that purpose. Pray for Him to expose what part you play in His greater plan and how that works into your life. I pray that God will open those doors for you to see it and feel it so clearly and that you will trust that obeying that calling will bring a joy that you did not know was possible.

When you feel confused, fearful, or the resistance is just too heavy and you begin to lose faith in God, remember that Jesus calms the storms. He calls us to have faith in what He has asked us to do, and He will take care of any chaos that stands in our way.

"Why are you fearful, O you of little faith?" Then he arose and rebuked the winds and the sea and there was great calm. (Matthew 8:26–27)

Can you imagine what a powerful and joyful world we would live in if we all followed our God-given purposes?

Let me leave you with this question. Can you imagine what a powerful and joyful world we would live in if we *all* followed our God-given purposes? If we all lived our lives seeking God's plan for each of us? What an impactful and loving world this would be if we all sought the joy that only He can give. You have talents. You have gifts. You have something special to offer this place. Don't waste your time here living mediocre. You are worth so much more than that.

> Before I formed you in the womb, I knew you. (Jeremiah 1:5)

> You are the light of the world. A city that is set on a hill cannot be hidden. Nor do they light a lamp and put it under a basket, but on a lampstand, and it gives light to all who are in the house. Let your light so shine before men that they may see your good works and glorify your Father in heaven. (Matthew 5:14–16)

ACKNOWLEDGMENTS

To some of my cheerleaders who have supported me since day one.

Gavin Filkins—the love of my life. The person who has seen the blood, sweat, and tears that have gone into this whole process to make this book a reality. The one who has had the most blind faith when he had no idea what was really happening in my heart. The person who has trusted the calling that I felt to pursue this journey when I sometimes did not. The one who never doubted me for a second. You have been more impactful than you will ever know. I love you, sweetheart.

Claudia Moore—my mama who raised me and helped me become the woman I am today. None of this would have been possible without the foundation you set for me and giving me everything you possibly could have throughout my entire life. You have always been my rock and a role model for how to live like Jesus.

April Bartle—my sweet sister who has been my hype girl since day one. Thank you for supporting this dream and for helping me stay confident in this calling. Your excitement in every step of this process inspired me to keep going when I doubted myself. Your enthusiasm has been crucial, and I am so thankful for you always being in my corner.

Angie Blank—one of the most beautiful souls I have ever met. The woman who listens to my crazy life, gives me spiritual advice, and makes me a better sister in Christ just through simple conversation—truly a spiritual mentor. You are amazing in every area, and I could not have done this without you.

Megan Rose—a dear friend who was a crucial part of this writing journey. Without you, this book would not have been written. You gave me the confidence to start with your kind words and constant encouragement. No matter where life takes you, never stop shining for Jesus and inspiring the world around you.

ABOUT THE AUTHOR

Amanda is a compassionate, determined, and resilient sister in Christ who yearns to follow the callings God has placed on her heart. She believes every single person has a God-given purpose, and she seeks to live hers out faithfully. She is a wife, sister, daughter, dog mama, and friend. She is a Midwest-living girl who loves to run, read, write, work on DIY projects, eat nourishing food, hang out with family, and spend time outside.

Amanda is passionate about health, which is why she obtained a bachelor's degree in exercise science and a master's degree in public health.

She loves deeply and she wears her heart on her sleeve. She hopes that through this book, readers are able to relate to her struggles and a desire to seek God's plan for their lives is passionately ignited.

9 781638 449041